AIDING AND ABETTING BY OMISSION:

Special Focus on Mode of Participation to the Crime of Extermination in the Rutaganira Case

AIDING AND ABETTING BY OMISSION:

Special Focus on Mode of Participation to the Crime of Extermination in the Rutaganira Case

Gracieux Mbuzukongira

GALDA VERLAG 2019

Bibliografische Information der Deutschen Nationalbibliothek
Die Deutsche Nationalbibliothek verzeichnet diese Publikation in der Deutschen Nationalbibliografie; detaillierte bibliografische Daten sind im Internet über http://dnb.ddb.de abrufbar.

ISBN 978-3-96203-098-8 (Print)
ISBN 978-3-96203-099-5 (E-book)

I have written this work not to teach men what they do not know,
but to remind them of what they already know
and is very evident to them, for you will find
in most of my words only things which most people know,
and concerning which they entertain
no doubts.

The RAMCHAL - Mesillat Yesharim (1707-1746)

TABLE OF CONTENTS

Acknowledgements....................xv

Introduction....................xix

Chapter 1: General theories on complicity as a mode of participation to a crime 1

1.1 Complicity through aiding and abetting 2

1.2 "Aiding and abetting" or "aiding or abetting" 3

1.3 Actus Reus 3

1.3.1 Practical assistance or moral support 4

1.3.2 The Threshold 5

1.3.3 Substantial contribution or any contribution by any other way 6

1.3.4 Substantial contribution or assisting otherwise 8

1.4 Mens rea 9

1.4.1 Conduct based intent 10

1.4.2 Consequence based intent 10

1.4.3 The mens rea test in Krnojelac Case 11

1.4.4. Causality 13

Chapter 2. Criminal Liability through command responsibility 15

2.1 Early States Practice 15

2.2 Legal Basis 17

2.3 Superior- Subordinate Relation 19

2.4 The Mental Element 21

2.5 Failure to prevent or to punish 24

Chapter 3. Inaction while under duty to act 27

3.1 Review of the jurisprudence of early tribunals 27

3.1.1 The Aleksovski Case 27

3.1.2 The Essen Lynching Case 28

3.1.3 The Jaluit Atoll Case 29

3.2 The Jurisprudence of the current ad-hoc tribunals 30

3.2.1 The Sainovic Case 30

3.2.2 The Ntagerura Case 33

3.3 Constitutive elements 34

3.3.1 The existence of a legal duty to act 34

3.3.2 Actus Reus 34

3.3.3 Mens Rea 35

3.3.4 Complicity by omission in the Rutaganira Case 36

3.3.5 Determination on the Actus Reus 36

3.3.6 Determination on the Mens Rea 48

Chapter 4: The Guilty Plea 51

4.1 Legal Basis 52

4.2 Advantage of the Guilty Plea 54

4.3 Validity of a Guilty Plea 55

4.3.1 Voluntariness 55

4.3.2 Inducement 56

4.3.3 The Threat 57

4.3.4 An informed Decision 59

4.4 The Rutaganira Guilty Plea 60

4.4.1 Unequivocal Plea 62

4.4.2 Sufficient Incriminating Facts 65

4.4.3 The Procedure 67

4.4.4 Rule 11bis of the Rules 70

4.5 The Sentencing Hearing 74

4.5.1 The Prosecution's Submission 75

4.5.2 The Defence Submission 76

Chapter 5. Crimes against Humanity 79

5.1 Historical Development 79

5.2 Development through the International Law Commission 80

5.3 Development through the Nuremberg Tribunal 83

5.4 Nexus Requirement to an Armed Conflict 84

5.5 Position of the Current Ad hoc Tribunals 85

5.5.1 Elements of the Crime 86

5.5.2 Murder 88

5.5.3. Extermination 90

Concluding Remarks: The Rutaganira Case 97

Selected Readings 99

Further Readings 103

Appendix: Case No. ICTR-95-1C-T 107

ACKNOWLEDGMENTS

This research has been conducted mainly at the Max-Planck-Institute for Comparative Public and International Law in Heidelberg, I take this opportunity to thank the Directors of the Institute, Professor Armin von Bogdandy and Professor Anne Peters for having opened the doors of the Institute for me once again and allowing me to carry out this research at the Institute.

In a special way I want to thank His Excellency Ambassador Mohammed Sani and Professor Mathias Sahinkuye of the African Institute of International Law in Arusha for having welcomed me at their Institute and having allowed me access at their various resources as well.

During this research I benefited from other scholars' contributions, in particular Professor Katja Ziegler of the School of Law of the University of Leicester and Professor Eki Omorogbe whose discussion at the beginning of this project was precious to me, I am forever grateful for the exchange we had.

I thank Colin Flinn for having accepted to proofread my draft and correct my grammar mistakes however any shortcomings shall remain exclusively mine.

My few years of academic profession have met high and low seasons. However Emeritus Bishop Professor Owdenburg Mdegella of the Evangelical Lutheran Church of Tanzania- Iringa Diocese has stood with me throughout. May you find my heartfelt thanks here, for having been such an inspiration.

I could not have carried out this research without the financial assistance I received from two German institutions namely the Max-Planck Gesellschaft and the Deutscher Akademischer Austauschdienst without which I could not have undertaken this research. However, in a special way, I wish to acknowledge the Max-Planck Gesellshaft.

I thank my family for having been supportive. I should start by thanking Reverend Anselme Shima Mbuzukongira who travelled to Heidelberg to whisper a word of comfort and a prayer in my favor when I was working on this research. I thank my wife Bébé L. Mahekay, who has always been there for us raising men and women worth the next generation.

Last, certainly not least, my friend Jaques Kotze of Cape Town, South Africa from whom I have received the most insightful reading materials.

INTRODUCTION

In its judgment of 14 March 2005, the International Criminal Tribunal of Rwanda (ICTR) in the case the Prosecutor v. Vincent Rutaganira, (the Rutaganira case), the Trial Chamber found the accused Vincent Rutaganira guilty of extermination as a crime against humanity in which he participated through complicity by omission.[1]

The Tribunal held that the accused aided and abetted the commission of the crime as he stood a few meters away from the place where the attackers assembled before and after the attacks. Thus, he was in a position to observe them as they assembled near his house and subsequently to know that attacks were being perpetrated on Mubuga Church, between 14th and 17th April 1994.[2]

Although in its judgment of 11 September 2006, in the Jean Mpambara case, the Trial Chamber held that evidence which is characterised as an omission can be used to show that an accused aided and abetted a crime, the Trial Chamber stressed that such liability is not automatic.

Indeed, the Trial Chamber held that it must be proven by showing that the accused's inaction had an encouraging or approving effect on the perpetrators; that the effect was substantial; and that the accused knew of this effect and of the perpetrator's criminal intention, albeit without necessarily sharing the perpetrators' criminal intent.[3]

---

[1] See ICTR, Vincent Rutaganira Trial Chamber Judgement, p 14

[2] Idem para 86

[3] See ICTR, Jean Mpambara Trial Chamber Judgement, para 22

The Trial Chamber further concluded that inaction without being present at the scene of a crime, was excluded from culpable omission.[4]

Whereas in its Judgment of 3rd March 2000 in the Tihomir Blaskic case, the Trial Chamber of the International Tribunal for the Prosecution of Persons Responsible for Serious Violations of International Humanitarian Law Committed in the Territory of the Former Yugoslavia Since 1991 (ICTY), held that the actus reus of aiding and abetting may be perpetrated through an omission, provided this failure to act has a decisive effect on the commission of the crime and that it is coupled with the requisite mens rea.[5]

Conversely, the Trial Chamber further found that the mere presence at the crime scene of a person with superior authority, such as a military commander, is a probative indication for determining whether that person encouraged or supported the perpetrators of the crime.[6]

The same ICTY in a different judgment on 15th March 2002, in the Milorad Krnojelac case, said that the presence alone at the scene of the crime is not conclusive of aiding and abetting unless it is demonstrated to have a significant legitimising or encouraging effect on the principal offender.[7]

The Trial Chamber ruled that it must be demonstrated that the aider and abeter carried out an act which consisted of practical assistance, encouragement or moral support to the principal offender.

The above examples provide an illustration of the challenge the ad hoc tribunals have faced when dealing with the concept of complicity by omission. Indeed while it is clear that aiding and abeting amount to a culpable encouragement to the commission of crimes, it is not clear which acts could amount to complicity by omission as a form of individual criminal liability.

[4] Idem para 23

[5] See ICTY, Tihomir Blaskic Trial Chamber Judgement, para 284, citing the authority of the judgements of Tadic Judgement, para. 686; Celebici Judgement, para. 842; and Akayesu Judgement, para. 705

[6] Idem para 284

[7] See ICTY, Milorad Krnojelac, Trial Judgement, para 89

This research intends to revisit the doctrine of participation to the commission of a crime through complicity as it seeks to determne under which circumstances could an omission trigger individual criminal responsibility of a participant for the crime committed by the principal offender.

The researchis therefore designed to contribute to the debate on the scope of the concept of complicity by omission and its prospects. A special focus will be given to the Rutaganira case in which the accused was found guilty of extermination as a crime against humanity to which he participated through complicity by omission.[8]

It should be noted in criminal law an omission can result ina crime on its own, as an act of omission could be considered as a mode of participation to a crime. Furthermore when omission is considered as a mode of participation, the law provides various situations in which such participation could trigger individual criminal responsibility.

For instance, a prison warden who has a duty to protect prisoners within the prison as their guarantor but who by omission lets criminals commit their crimes against prisoners who are under his guard. A commanding officer who fails to stop or punish their subordinate from committing a crime will be held accountable for such omission under the principle of command responsibility.

These types of omission arehowever different from the situation where a given authority is present at the scene of a crime which is committed by individuals who are not necessarily their subordinates, even though it remains debatable whether the presence is an act or an omission as it might require an act of movement.

It should be indicated that as far as reseach methods is concerned, this research will take two approaches: a theoretical approach reflecting of the actual creation of legal rules; and an implementation focused approach, reflecting on the observance and application of legal rules and the successes achieved in strengthening legality and for consolidating law.[9]

---

[8] See ICTR,Vincent Rutaganira, Judgement and Sentence, p 14
[9] See Dzhangir Kerimov, Methology of Law, Progress Publishers, 1989, p 12

As defined by Banakar and Travers[10], the rule-based paradigm which consists of a study of a law with recourse to the exegesis authoritative argument that allows to read and criticize its content will be of great use for this research.

The study's focus will be doctrinal, analysing legal sources available within the United Nations Mechanism for International Criminal Tribunals (UN-MICT) and its valuable resources. The research will also be based on other sources, especially scholarly writings published in leading international and national periodicals, journals, newspapers, reports, Aide-Mémoire, Travaux Préparatoires, reference works and other relevant data available.

The following chapter intends to discuss the concept of complicity as a mode of participation in a crime and its various application.

[10] Reza Banakar and Max Travers, Law, Sociology and Method, Theory and Method in Socio-Legal Research, Hart Publishing, 2005, p 8

CHAPTER 1

GENERAL THEORIES ON COMPLICITY AS A MODE OF PARTICIPATION TO A CRIME

It will be recalled that in the history of international criminal prosecution the Nuremberg War Crimes Tribunalnever made a differentiation in the concept of criminal participation,[11] that is, the tribunal never made a distinction based on role and kind of contribution the accused made to the commission of the crime. It followed that participant were tried and sentenced equally as principal perpetrators.

In as much as in the Germain Katanga case the Trial Chamber said that "it is not precluded that having adjudged guilt, a bench may choose to mete out mitigated penalties to accessories, although to do so is not peremptory."[12] Furthermore, though current tribunals and the ICC have made such a distinction in their procedings, such distinction does not warrant a lesser penalty.

Indeed the Statute of the ICC[13] read jointly with the Rules of Procedure and Evidence[14] at the ICC do not take into account the mode of participation when sentencing. It is in this spirit that in the Germain Katanga case, the court

[11] See Elies Van Sliedregt, Individual criminal responsibility in international law, Oxford University Press, 2012, p 35
[12] See ICC, Germain Katanga Trial Judgement, para 1386
[13] See Article 78 of the Rome Statute
[14] See Rule 145

indicted that"a person responsible as an instigator, for the purposes of article 25(3)(b), may incur a penalty akin or even identical to that handed down against a person found responsible as a perpetrator of the same crime."

The Trial Chamber further said: "The fact remains that neither the Statute nor the Rules of Procedure and Evidence prescribe a rule for the mitigation of penalty for forms of liability other than commission and the Chamber sees no automatic correlation between mode of liability and penalty."[15]

It is not surprising that calls have been to end the mode of liability for international crimes.[16] Nevertheless the purpose of international criminal justice goes beyond a mere distribution of sentences, as it also serves as record keeper for the future generation; it remains relevant that every individual is held accountable for the crime according to their participation in it.

1.1 Complicity through Aiding and Abetting

In general terms the concept of complicity applies when a person without being the principal offender "the perpetrator" has rendered assistance to the commission of the crime. Statutes of the ICTY and the ICTR respectively in their articles 7(1) and 6(1) contain a similar provision according to which: „A person who planned, instigated, ordered, committed or otherwise aided and abetted in the planning, preparation or execution of a crime [...] shall be individually responsible for the crime."

According toarticle 25 (3)(c) of the Rome Statute: "For the purpose of facilitating the commission of such a crime, aids, abets or otherwise assists in its commission or its attempted commission, including providing the means for its commission."

[15] See ICC, Germain Katanga Trial Judgement, para 1387

[16] See James G. Stewart, The end of "Modes of Liability" for international Crimes" in Leiden Journal of international Law, Vol. 25, 2012, pp 165-219

1.2 "Aiding and Abetting" or "Aiding or Abetting"

Though the meaning of the concepts aiding and abetting might be closely connected, in the Akayesu Case the ICTR defined the term aiding and abetting as follows, "Aiding means giving assistance to someone. Abetting, on the other hand, would involve facilitating the commission of an act by being sympathetic thereto."[17] Thus as said by Gideon Baos," the phrase 'aiding and abetting' refers to two discrete activities.[18]

It couldbe indicated that the conjuction "and" in aiding and abetting does not have a cumulative effect in this context. Indeed either of the two concepts if separated could satify the court for the participation of the accused. Luckuly no court has ventured in to this adventure as courts have considered one aspect suffient to triger individual responsibility in which context one would rather this participation to be refered to as aiding or abetting.

It is in that line that the in the Kunarac case the Trial Chamber found that: "The contribution of an aider and abettor may take the form of practical assistance, encouragement or moral support which has a substantial effect on the perpetration of the crime."[19] A better understanding of the concept requires that the actus reus and the mens rea are discussed separately.

1.3 Actus Reus

The Furundzija Judgement contains the most cited definition of the concept of aiding and abetting. The Trial Chamber indicated that: "In aiding and abetting the objective element is constituted by practical assistance, encouragement, or moral support by the accessory to the principal in addition such assistance must have a substantial effect on the perpetration of the crime."[20]

[17] See ICTR, Jean Paul Akayesu Trial Judgement, para 484

[18] See Gideon Boas, 'Omission Liability in International Criminal Law - A Case for Reform', in Shane Darcy and Joseph Powderly, Judicial Creativity at the International Criminal Tribunals, Oxford University Press, 2011, 204-226

[19] See ICTY, Kunarac et al. Trial Judgement, 391

[20] See ICTY, Anto Furundjiza Trial Judgement, para 235, the same definition can be found in Antonio Cassese, international criminal law, oup, 2003, p 188. Needless to point out that the author of the cited source was equally seating on the bench which delivered the landmark judgement cited above

Thus the actus reus needed for the participation to a crime by way of aiding and abetting is double folded. That is a practical assistance or moral support on the one hand and a requirement that such assistance or support has an effect on the perpetration of the crime[21] on the other hand. A combination of these two factors will satisfy the requirement of the actus reus for aiding and abetting.

1.3.1 Practical Assistance or Moral Support

1.3.1.1 Practical Assistance

No definition of practical assistance exists in international law. However the existing jurisprudence has established that such assistance include "all acts of assistance by words or acts that lend encouragement or support, as long as the requisite intent is present."[22] The same definition was adopted by the Trial Chamber in the Kajelijeli Case as it found that aiding and abetting "relates to acts of assistance that intentionally provide encouragement or support to the commission of a crime."[23]

It is equally settled that such assistance may take place before, during or after the crime. One may cite for example a driver who picks up criminals to evacuate them from the crime scene, thus bringing in assistance after the commission. Considering that the fact that these criminals knew they would be evacuated from the scene might have been a determinant factor which substantially contributed to their decision to commit the crime.

Such assistance given by the participant has reached the level of triggering their individual criminal responsibility albeit as accessorial to the commission of the crime.

---

[21] Jessie Ingle, Aiding and abetting by omission before the International Criminal tribunals, in Journal of International Criminal Justice, Vol 14. No. 3, 2016, p 749

[22] See ICTY, Dusco Tadic Trial Judgement, para 689

[23] See ICTR, Juvenal Kajelijeli Trial Judgement, para 766

1.3.1.2 Moral Support

Moral support can be considered as having substantially contributed to the commission of a crime. A decision made by a domestic court in the Bouloc Case, provides a better illustration of moral support. In this case the physical presence of a man at the time his female partner commits abortion was considered as moral support which substantially contributed to the commission of the crime.[24]

Thus any behaviour, act, words or gesture is relevant provided that behaviour contributes in a decisive manner to the determination of a person to commit a crime. Such encouragement coupled with the required mens rea could trigger individual criminal responsibility as accomplice.

This is in the line of the Trial Chamber in the Blasic case as it found that:

> [A]iding and abetting need not assume the provision of tangible or practical assistance but may also consist in giving encouragement or moral or psychological support to the perpetrator of the crime through words or attitude or even by merely being present at the crime scene.[25]

1.3.2 The Threshold

Even though the concept of threshold is not defined, for any assistance to cause criminal responsibility, such assistance must substantially contribute to the commission of the crime. The ICTY dealt with the concept of aiding and abetting for the first time in the Tadic case, it was however in the Furundzija case the concept was more elaborated.

After having reviewed various cases at domestic level, including the Einsatzgruppen and Zyklon B cases in which it was held that "the relationship

---

[24] See Jerue v Alaska, 1994 WL 16196278 as Cited by Christopher Gosnell, Damned if you don't: Liability for omission in international criminal law, Ashgate research companion, 2013, p 114

[25] See ICTY, Tihomir Blasic Trial Judgement, para 271, The same view is shared by the Trial Chamber in the DuscoTadic case which found that: aiding and abetting includes all acts of assistance by words or acts that lend encouragement or support. See ICTY, Dusco Tadic Trial Judgement, para 689

between the acts of the accomplice and of the principal must be such that the acts of the accomplice make a significant difference to the commission of the criminal act by the principal."[26]

The Trial Chamber then concluded that: "The position under customary international law seems therefore to be best reflected in the proposition that the assistance must have a substantial effect on the commission of the crime."[27]

The same reasoning was followed in Musema case when the Tribunal emphasized that "any act of participation must substantially contribute to the commission of the crime."[28] Further the Tribunal said that the aider and abettor assists or facilitates another in the accomplishment of a substantive offence.[29]

It should be pointed out that the Rome Statute seems to have introduced a lower shreshold for participation as per its article 25(3)(d) as discussed below.

1.3.3 Substantial Contribution or any Contribution by any other Way

Article 25(3) (d) set the lowest standard of participation to crime in international law providing that: "A person shall be criminally responsible and liable for punishment for a crime within the jurisdiction of the Court if that person: In any other way contributes to the commission or attempted commission of such a crime by a group of persons acting with a common purpose..."

It is in this respect that the victim's Legal Representative in the Germain Katanga case submitted that, criminal liability could be triggered under this

[26] See ICTY, Anto Furundjiza Trial Judgement, para 233
[27] Idem
[28] See ICTR, Alfred Musema Trial Judgement, para 126
[29] Idem

article even when the conduct of the accused is "not unlawful or substantial."[30] The Trial Chamber found that under article 25(3)(d), liability is attracted by participation "in any other way" and that this provision creates a residual form of accessorial participation.

Such form of participation which might not meet the standard of accessorial participation provided for under article 25(3)(c) according to which: "For the purpose of facilitating the commission of such a crime, aids, abets or otherwise assists in its commission or its attempted commission, including providing the means for its commission."

The Court went on by saying that a significant contribution, attributed to each crime, must be proven beyond a reasonable doubt. A contribution to the crime must bea significant contribution, and thus the Chamber wished to lay stress on a contribution which may influence the commission of the crime. Inconsequential conduct and immaterial to the commission of the crime cannot, therefore, be considered sufficient and constitute a contribution within the meaning of article 25(3)(d) of the Statute.[31]

This position matches the position that the ICC held in the Callixte Mbarushimana case. Indeed, the Pre-Trial Chamber found that it would have been inappropriate for such liability to be incurred through any contribution to a group crime. The PTC further said: "not only crimes, but also contributions to crimes need to reach a certain threshold of significance in order to be within the Court's ambit."[32]

The reasoning of the Pre-Trial Chamber was that "such a threshold is necessary to exclude contributions which, because of their level or nature, were clearly not intended by the drafters of the Statute to give rise to individual criminal responsibility."

---

[30] See ICC, Germain Katanga TrialJudgement, para 1614
[31] Idem, para 1632
[32] See ICC, Callixte Mbarushimana Pre-Trial Judgement, para276

It further explained that many members of a community may provide contributions to a criminal organisation in the knowledge of the group's criminality without reaching the required level of threshold which could trigger their criminal liability.

Such case would include landlords, grocers, pharmacists, taxi drivers... who would do anything which contributes to a group committing international crimes. Thus the Pre Trial Chamber considered that 25(3)(d) liability would become overextended if any contribution were sufficient.[33]

1.3. 4 Substantial Contribution or Assisting Otherwise

The prescription of Article 25(3)(c) indicates that an accomplice could "otherwise assist" the commission of the crime. The use of the term "otherwise" does not mean that the participation of the accused is not substantial, rather the opposite.[34] The approach of the court and tribunals has been on a case by case basis.

For instance, in the Jean Pierre Bemba case the Court held that in comparing article 25(3)(a) and (b) the Statute implies a lower degree of blameworthiness in the sense that on the one hand the co-perpetrator could frustrate the commission of the offence by not performing their task, or they directly commit the prohibited acts, while the accessorial participant under Article 25(3)(c) assists the commission of an offence by the perpetrator(s).[35]

Obviously the higher threshold is reached when the accused commits the material element of the crime. This was demonstrated in the Bemba case where Mr Arido, was charged with having committed crimes against the administration of justice as provided for underarticle 70(1)(c) of the Statute, a

---

[33] Idem, para 277

[34] Kai Ambos, Modes of criminal responsibility, in Max Planck Encyclopaedia of International Law, 2013

[35] See ICC, Jean-Pierre Bemba Gomba et al. Public Redacted Version of Judgment pursuant to Article 74 of the Statute, 19 October 2016, para 85-6

crime to which he was charged as having participated through article 25(3)(a) as a perpetrator, in the alternative, the accused was charged of the same crime provided for under article 70(1)(c) however with article 25(3)(c) as mode of participation that aiding and abetting.[36]

Mr Arido was accused of having recruited D-2, D-3, D-4 and D-6 and intentionally promised them money and relocation in Europe in exchange for their testimony in the main case. Furthermore, Mr Arido was said to have intentionally instructed and briefed the four witnesses (or facilitated their briefing by others) to present themselves as military men to Mr Kilolo and the Court even while believing that they did not have such a background.[37]

The court convicted Mr. Arido as principal perpetrator of the crime against administration of justice and refrained from looking into a finding of the alternative mode of participation through aiding and abetting,[38] pursuant article 70(1)(c) of the Statute according to which: "The Court shall have jurisdiction over the following offences against its administration of justice when committed intentionally Corruptly influencing a witness, obstructing or interfering with the attendance or testimony of a witness, retaliating against a witness for giving testimony or destroying, tampering with or interfering with the collection of evidence."

1.4 Mens Rea

Article 30(1) of the Rome Statute sets out the mental element of a crime as the first legal expression of the concept of mens rea in international criminal law. It provides that: "Unless otherwise provided, a person shall be criminally responsible and liable for punishment for a crime within the jurisdiction of the Court only if the material elements are committed with intent and knowledge."

---

[36] Idem, para 943
[37] Idem, para 944
[38] Idem, para 945

From the reading of the above cited article one could conclude that article 30(1) requires two cumulative elements for the purposes of satisfying means rea of the accomplice. The two elements are the intention and the knowledge of the accomplice to participate in the crime of which he is not a perpetrator. In other words, the accomplice must know and share the dolus nocendi of the principal.

Article 30(2) explains further how the concept intent is understood by saying:

> For the purposes of this article, a person has intent where:
> (a) In relation to conduct, that person means to engage in the conduct;
> (b) In relation to a consequence, that person means to cause that consequence or is aware that it will occur in the ordinary course of events.

1.4.1 Conduct Based Intent

The state of mind of a person could be shown from their conduct. That is to say that series of certain behaviours could lead the court to understand the intent of the actor at the time they committed their acts.

This could be the case of a participant who drives away the principal offender after they have committed a crime, avoiding any possible route where they could be intercepted by the police; it could be said that the participant had driven them away for the purposes of hiding them from facing justice.

1.4.2 Consequence Based Intent

Noticeably, article 30(2)(b) is double folded; it applies to the case whereby an accused meant the result of their behaviour generally referred to as dolus nocendi. As said by Antonio Cassese citing the District Court of Tel Aviv, "it is a well know rule that any person in his right mind is held to intend the natural consequences of his action."[39]

The key element in the second layer of the same article is the awareness that if all things remaining unchanged, the harm will be caused. Such intent will be demonstrated by the forseability of the consequences of the conduct of the accused.[40]

For instance, a parent who locks a child inside a house which is on fire could be said to have intended the death of that child. Considering that the death of such child is a forseable consequence of such act. Thus any one who could assist such parent may be charged for participation to such crime.

Thus article 30(2)(b) provides for a possibility that the person might have either meant the consequence of their act or alternatively was aware that such consequences will be the result of their conduct. It is in that line that when discussing the mens rea in the Furundzija Case, the Trial Chamber said that:

> With regard to mens rea, the Trial Chamber must determine whether it is necessary for the accomplice to share the mens rea of the principal or whether mere knowledge that his actions assist the perpetrator in the commission of the crime is sufficient to constitute mens rea in aiding and abetting the crime. The case law indicates that the latter will suffice.[41]

1.4.3 The Mens Rea Test in Krnojelac Case

The facts of this case are as follows. Mr Milorad Krnojelac held a position of warden at the Fo~a Kazneno-Popravni Dom prison facility.[42] As warden

[39] Antonio Cassese, International Criminal Law, Oxford University Press, 2003, p 163
[40] See ICTY, Dusco Tadic Trial Judgement, para. 674; See ICTY, Celebici Trial Judgement, para. 326; See ICTY, Zlatko Aleksovski Trial Judgement, para. 61
[41] See ICTY, Anto Furundjiza Trial Judgement, para 236
[42] See ICTY, Milorad Krnojelac Trial Judgement para 96

he was the highest administrative authority of the prison and exercised the supervision of prison activities as its manager[43] at the time that crimes which gave rise to this case were committed, including persecution, torture and beating, willful killing, murder etc.[44]

Without him perpetrating any of the indicated crimes, the Trial Chamber made a finding that he was an accompliceto the crimes which were committed in the prison at the time he was warden; as accomplice to such crimes he was convicted as aider and abettor.

The Trial Chamber held that the "Accused was aware of the intent of the principal offenders and that he was aware that his failure to take any action as warden in relation to this knowledge contributed in a substantial way to the continued maintenance of these conditions constituting inhumane acts and cruel treatment by the principal offenders by giving encouragement to the principal offenders to maintain these living conditions"[45]

This position was again confirmed in the Ngirabatware Case. The Appeals Chamber said that the requisite mens rea for aiding and abetting is knowledge that the acts performed by the aider and abettor assist the commission of the specific crime of the principal perpetrator.

The aider and abettor need not share the mens rea of the principal perpetrator but must be aware of the essential elements of the crime ultimately committed by the principal, including his state of mind.[46]

It should be noted though that in the Ngirabatware case, the Appeals Chamber might be seen as having raised the standard of awareness slightly higher in requiring the knowledge of the specific crime and the state of the mind of the principal. Indeed such level of awareness needs to be maintained for specific crimes which require a specific intention like genocide.

---

[43] Idem para 97
[44] See ICTY, Milorad Krnojelac, indictment
[45] See ICTY, Milorad Krnojelac Trial Judgement para 171
[46] See ICTR, Augustin Ngirabatware Appeals Judgement, para 155

In the remaining situations, without having the precise knowledge of the offence, if the accomplice is in anyway aware of essential elements of the crime and acts in support of the commission of the crime, such participation could still satisfy the means rea.

1.4.4 Causality

In general terms, in order to establish criminal responsibility of the accused, the tribunal must establish the link that exists between the conduct of the accused and the result of the crime they are accused of. However such rule cannot apply to a participant to a crime since they did not commit any material element of the crime, least they become coperpetrators.[47]

Thus, the jurisprudence of international tribunals has established that there must not be a causality link between the act of the accomplice and the result of the crime[48] they are accused of having participated in. It needs to be stressed that the substantiality of the participation of the accomplice is rather relevant as far as the determination of the principal to commit the crime is concerned.

In other words, after the accomplice participation has contributed to the decision of the principal to commit the crime the court is required to check to what extent has such participation contributed to the result of the crime.[49] This explains why the accomplice could still be held criminally responsible even in a case where their assistance has not been of use during the commission of the crime.

This position is understandable since the law intends to punish the conduct of the participant not the result of the crime. Thus a driver who agrees to

---

[47] Hector Olasolo and Enrique Carnero Rojo, Forms of accessorial Liability under Art 25(3) and (c), in Carsten Stahn, The law and practice of the international criminal court, Oxford University Press, 2015, p580-1

[48] See ICTY, Kunaric et al. Trial Judgement, para 391

[49] See ICTY, Tihomir Blasic Trial Judgement, para 285 the same position was restated in the same case by the Appeals Chamber, see ICTY, Tihomir Blasic Appeals Judgement, para 48

facilitate the escape of the principal after the commission of the crime will still be held accountable even if after having committed the crime the principal walked back home without the intended offence being committed.

The responsibility of this driver is not based on the fact that their assistance was used or not rather that they contributed in a substantial way to the decision of the principal to commit the crime. It is in that line that international tribunals have affirmed that participation may occur before, during or after the commission of the crime.[50]

[50] See ICTR, Juvenal Kajelijeli Trial Judgement, para 766

CHAPTER 2

CRIMINAL LIABILITY THROUGH COMMAND RESPONSIBILITY

2.1 Early States Practice

The Statutes of the International Military Tribunals of Nuremberg and Tokyo didn't have a specific legal provision on command responsibility. This doctrine developed as a matter of states practice and later became captured by future treaties and statutes. For instance, Article IX of the Chinese Law of 24th October, 1946, Governing the Trial of War Criminals, stated that:

> Persons who occupy a supervisory or commanding position in relation to war criminals and in their capacity as such have not fulfilled their duty to prevent crimes from being committed by their subordinates shall be treated as the accomplices of such war criminals.[51]

Whereas the Dutch metropolitan law, in its Article 27(a) paragraph 3 of the Extraordinary Penal Law Decree of 22nd December, 1943 provided that "any superior who deliberately permits a subordinate to be guilty" of a war crime or crime against humanity is liable to the same punishment as the perpetrator.

[51] See Law report of trials of war criminals selected and prepared by the United Nations War Crimes Commission, Vol. XIV, 1949, p. 158.

Furthermore, Article 9 of the Netherlands East Indies Statute Book Decree No. 45 of 1946 stated that:

> He whose subordinate has committed a war crime shall be equally punishable for that war crime, if he has tolerated its commission by his subordinate whilst knowing, or at least must have reasonably supposed, that it was being or would be committed.[52]

Such regulations were equally reflected in the case law which was developed in the aftermath of the Second World War.

Thus, in the case of Lieutenant-General Baba Masao of 28th May to 2nd June 1947, before The Australian Military Court, Rabaul where General Masao was charged of having unlawfully disregarded and failed to discharge his duty as commander to control the conduct of the members of his command whereby they committed brutal atrocities when General Masao was commander of armed forces of Japan, the Court found that criminal liability of a commander may result from offences committed by their troops.

The reasoning of the Court was that such "criminal negligeance" may appear as "wilful negligence if the commander is aware of atrocities being committed by his troops and fails to prevent them, or it may be constituted by the performance of a field commander's duties with such culpable neglect as to display indifference as to whether or not offences are committed by the troops."[53]

Further the Judge Advocate highlighted that: "In order to succeed the prosecution must prove . . . that war crimes were committed as a result of the accused's failure to discharge his duties as a commander, either by deliberately failing in his duties or by culpably or willfully disregarding them, not caring whether this resulted in the commission of a war crime or not."[54]

Another example could be the case of General Tomoyuki Yamashita at the United State Military Commission, Manila, from 8th October to 7th December 1945 and the Supreme Court of the United States of America where General Yamashita was tried for offences committed by his troops.

---

[52] Idem, Vol. XI, pp 100-1
[53] Idem, p 60
[54] Idem, p 60

General Yamashita was Commanding General of the Fourteenth Army Group of the Imperial Japanese Army in the Philippine Islands. He was charged with "unlawfully disregarding and failing to discharge his duty as commander to control the acts of members of his command by permitting them to commit war crimes."

At his trial the Court wanted to know the extent to which a commander of troops can be held liable for offences committed by troops under his command which he did not ordered, on the grounds that he ought to have used his authority to prevent their being committed or their continued perpetration, or that he must, taking into account all the circumstances, be presumed to have either ordered or condoned the offences.[55]

The Court found that it was clearly established that a responsibility may arise in the absence of any direct proof of the giving of an order for the commission of crimes.[56] The Court cited the case of Yuicki Sakamoto, where Mr. Sakamoto was sentenced to life imprisonment after being found guilty of having failed to discharge his duty as Commanding Officer thus permitting his subordinates to commit cruel and brutal atrocities against prisoners of war.[57]

2.2 Legal Basis

Article 86(2) of the first addition protocol to the Geneva Conventions providing for the duty of commanders says:

> The fact that a breach of the Conventions or of this Protocol was committed by a subordinate does not absolve his superiors from penal or disciplinary responsibility, as the case may be, if they knew, or had information which should have enabled them to conclude in thecircumstances at the time, that he was committing or was going to commit such a breach and if they did not take all feasible measures within their power to prevent or repress the breach.[58]

[55] Idem, Vol IV, p 84

[56] Idem, p 85

[57] Idem, p 86

[58] The commentary of this article has explained the relationship that exists between ranks and responsibilities. It further explained how the regime itself is inseparable with the status of armed forces perhaps this would justify the requirement of the 1907 Hague Convention according

Indeed the International Law Commission in its work has continuously discussed the issue for instance article 6 of its 1996 report stipulates that:

> The fact that a crime against the peace and security of mankind was committed by a subordinate does not relieve his superiors of criminal responsibility, if they knew or had reason to know, in the circumstances at the time, that the subordinate was committing or was going to commit such a crime and if they did not take all necessary measures within their power to prevent or repress the crime.

It's no wonder that the principle of command responsibility is well settled in international criminal justice. It is further couched in articles 6/7(3) of the statutes of the ICTR and ICTY according saying that:

> The fact that any of the acts … was committed by a subordinate does not relieve his or her superior of criminal responsibility if he or she knew or had reason to know that the subordinate was about to commit such acts or had done so and the superior failed to take the necessary and reasonable measures to prevent such acts or to punish the perpetrators thereof.

The same is captured in the Rome Statute under article 28(a) providing that:

> A military commander or person effectively acting as a military commander shall be criminally responsible for crimes within the jurisdiction of the Court committed by forces under his or her

---

to which: "The laws, rights, and duties of war apply not only to armies, but also to militia and volunteer corps fulfilling the following conditions:

1. To be commanded by a person responsible for his subordinates;
2. To have a fixed distinctive emblem recognizable at a distance;
3. To carry arms openly; and
4. To conduct their operations in accordance with the laws and customs of war…

See article 1 of the Annex to the Convention (VI) respecting the Laws and Customs of War on Land and its annex: Regulations concerning the Laws and Customs of War on Land. The Hague, 18 October 1907

> effective command and control, or effective authority and control as the case may be, as a result of his or her failure to exercise control properly over such forces.

International jurisprudence has developed a considerable body of case law according to which the requirements of the criminal responsibility of the commanding or superior officer are met when the following conditions are satisfied:

- Superior-Subordinate Relationship
- Knowing or Having Reason to Know
- Failing to Prevent or Punish

2.3 Superior- Subordinate Relation

The existence of the superior-subordinate relationship is a conditio sine qua non for the application of the principle of command responsibility. From the existing international jurisprudence, it could be submitted that command or superior would refer to the person "who possesses the power or authority in either a de jure or a de facto form to prevent a subordinate's crime or to punish the perpetrators of the crime after the crime is committed."[59]

It should be stressed that it is immaterial whether such superior officer is indeed a commanding officer within the line of the chain of command of armed forces or a civilian. Making reference to Article 87 (1) AP (1) which specifically provides for duties of commanders the commentary of Article 86 (2) has clarified that the use of the concept of superiors is broader and should be seen in terms of a hierarchy encompassing the concept of control.[60]

---

[59] See ICTY, Celebici Case Appeals Judgement, para 192
[60] See Commentary of article 86 Additional Protocol 1

Thus, the principle will apply to whoever had the ability to prevent the commission of the crime or to punish it after it had occurred. This could be a military commanding office within the formal line of command as it could be any other officer would it be a member of the armed forces or a civilian authority who exercises their powers either in a de jure or de facto fashion.

Such criminal responsibility does not arise from the qualification of the accused rather than the powers and effective control they exercised on the perpetrator of the crime. How such power was obtained becomes immaterial. The court will rather satisfy itself that the accused had powers to prevent the perpetrator from committing the crime or if they had powers to punish the perpetrator after the commission of the crime.

The case of Zejnil Delalic and others which is refered to as the Celebici Case raised the question of a formally appointed authority but who indeed does not exercise such powers.

In the case of Wilhelm List and others, famously known as the Hostages Trial before the United States Military Tribunal, Nuremberg from 8th July, 1947 to 19th February, 1948, the Tribunal held that the commanding general cannot defend themselves on the ground that a unit was taking unlawful orders from someone other than themselves who should be subsequently held responsible for command responsibility of such crimes.

For instance, some co-accused in the Wilhelm Case submitted that some SS units were under the direct command of Heinrich Rimmler from whom they received direct orders. They claimed that some crimes were committed without their knowledge, consent or approval.[61] The Tribunal however said that a commanding general cannot hide behind a puppet government and plead that he is not responsible for their acts.[62]

[61] See Law report of trials of war criminals selected and prepared by the United Nations War Crimes Commission Vol VIII, 1949, p 69

[62] Idem, p 89

However the Celebici Case might have departed from the Hostages Trial. Indeed, in the Celebici Case the Tribunal found that criminal responsibility is triggered on the factual basis, a de jure authority who didn't exercise their control over their subordinates might not be held account under this mode of liability, without excluding a possibility of finding another mode of liability.

Nevertheless as indicated the Celebici Case, it the onus will be on the accused to demonstrate to the court that they indeed were not in command of the perpetrator at the time of the commission of the crimes.[63]

The Bagilishema Case raised a pertinent question of a superior or commander who is administratively responsible for a geographic region, however without exercising his authority on individual persons who commit crimes. The Trial Chamber found that "the essential element is not whether a superior had authority over a certain geographical area, but whether he or she had effective control over the individuals who committed the crimes."[64]

2.4 The Mental Element

In the trial of Erhard Milch before the United States, Military Tribunal at Nuremberg of 20th December 1946 to 17th April 1047, the Tribunal found the accused not guilty[65] for crimes which were committed by people within his command because his relation to the perpetrator was too remote to make him responsible for their acts.

---

[63] See ICTY, Celebici Case, Trial Judgement, para 405

[64] See ICTR, Ignace Bagilishema Trial Judgement, para 45

[65] See Law report of trials of war criminals selected and prepared by the United Nations War Crimes Commission, Vol VII, 1949, p 37

During Second World War Mr. Erhard Milch was Inspector-General and a Field-Marshal in the German Air Force, Aircraft Master General, Member of the Central Planning Board and Chief of the Jaegerstab. Amongst other things he was accused of illegal experiments against prisoners of war.

At his trial, the Tribunal found evidence that the accused participated in or instituted the experiments, or that they were conducted under his direction. Neither was there any proof of his knowledge that unwilling subjects would be forced to submit to experiments or that they would be painful and dangerous to human life.[66]

In its judgment, the Tribunal citing the Pohl Case, where the accused Erwin Tschentscher, who was a battalion commander of a supply column, and a company commander, on the Russian Front during 1941, was not found responsible for the murder of Jewish civilians and other non-combatants in Poland and the Ukraine by members of his commands because the Tribunal found that he had no "actual knowledge" of these offences.[67]

Thus the Tribunal found Milch was found not guilty under this count because the Tribunal was not satisfied that he knew of the illegal nature of the experiments carried out by persons in his command.

It follows that the means rea requirement of the application of the command responsibility is that the commanding officer knew or should have known about the commission of the crime. Indeed, Article 7(3) of the Rome Statute indicates that a superior may incur criminal responsibility for criminal acts of subordinates “if he knew or had reason to know that the subordinate was about to commit such acts or had done so” but fails to prevent such acts or punish such subordinate.

---

[66] Idem, p 34

[67] Idem, pp. 63-64

A better understanding of this article would require a joint reading with the above cited Article 86 (2). From this, one could conclude that a superior would be considered to know about the crime within the meaning of Article 7 (3) of the Rome Statute, if they had actual information about the commission of the crime, as per Article 86 (2) AP (1). In other words the superior was in possession of the information about the crime.

Furthermore, one may submit that there is some information which is considered to be known by any superior by the virtue of their position. Such information will include the tactical facts, without which one cannot lead the troop and will always be considered as such.

In addition, if a superior received non conclusive information about the commission of a crime, they are under a duty to enquire, and if they fail to do so, they could be considered to have known about the commission of the crime.

It still remains less clear in which other situation the superior could be considered to have had reason to know about the commission of the crime within the meaning of Article 86 (2) AP (1). If one may make reference to the French version according to which:

> Le fait qu'une infraction ... a été commise par un subordonné n'exonère pas ses supérieurs de leur responsabilité pénale ... s'ils savaient ou possédaient des informations leur permettant de conclure ... que ce subordonné commettait ou allait commettre une telle infraction

It becomes clear that whereas the English version says that if the superior "had information which should have enabled them to conclude," the French version is more direct by providing that if they "had information enabling them to conclude..."

For instance such conclusion can be reached if there are reports[68] addressed to the accused on the matter, if the widespread of the commission of the crime was of such a scale that they should have put they on notice that such crimes are being committed in area under their jurisdiction…

Thus as explained by the International Law Commission, the phrase 'had reason to know' should be understood as having the same meaning as the phrase 'had information enabling them to conclude' which is used in the Additional Protocol I.[69]

2.5 Failure to prevent or to punish

As already referred in General Yamashita Case who was charged for crimes committed by his subordinates, during his trial, the submitted at the time of the commission of crimes which gave rise to the case, the accused was not in control of his subordinate as the channel of command had been seriously disrupted to the extent that the accused had no control whatsoever on the perpetrators.[70]

Interestingly the Commission and the Court found him guilty even though it was never established that he was in full command of his troops when they committed such crimes.

However in his dissenting opinion, Justice Murphy said that " to use the very inefficiency and disorganisation created by the victorious forces as the primary basis for condemning officers of the defeated armies bears no resemblance to justice or to military reality."

Justice Murphy continues to say that international law does not impose liability for failure to meet the ordinary responsibilities of command under

[68] See Commentary Additional Protocol 1
[69] See Yearbook of the International Law Commission, A/CN.4/SER. A/1996
[70] See Law report of trials of war criminals selected and prepared by the United Nations War Crimes Commission, Vol VII, 1949, p18

circumstances that they cannot discharge such duties.[71] Justice Rutledge, dissenting, went further by stating that considering all state of things the accused had been convicted for a crime "in which knowledge is an essential element, with no proof of knowledge other than what would be inadmissible in any other capital case or proceeding."[72]

It needs to be stressed that current practice seems to depart from the Yamashita judgment, for instance in the Jean Pierre Bemba Gombo Case, the Trial Chamber found the accused guilty of crimes committed by members of his rebellious armed group when he sent them into the Republic of Central Africa to fight side by side with the RCA governmental forces which was fighting against its own rebellion.

The Appeals Chamber however reversed the Trial Chamber's judgement and acquitted Mr. Bemba stating that the Trial Chamber did not demonstrate how the commander did not take specific and concrete measures that were available to him which a reasonably diligent commander in comparable circumstances would have taken.[73]

The Trial Chamber further states that the accused's troops were operating in a foreign country with the attendant difficulties on Mr Bemba's ability, as a remote commander, to take appropriate measures[74] as he faced logistical difficulties in conducting investigations which had to be overcome.[75]

The Appeals Chamber found that the Trial Chamber erred by failing to properly appreciate the limitations that Mr. Bemba would have faced in investigating and prosecuting crimes as a remote commander sending troops to a foreign country.[76]

[71] See Law report of trials of war criminals selected and prepared by the United Nations War Crimes Commission, Vol VII, p 51
[72] Idem, p 60
[73] See ICC, Jean-Bemba Gombo, Appeals Judgement, para 170
[74] Idem, para 171
[75] Idem, para 172
[76] Idem, para 189

The reasoning of the Appeals Chamber's judgement seems to align with the International Law Commission decision according to which for the superior to incur responsibility, he must have had the legal competence to take measures to prevent or repress the crime and the material possibility to take such measures.[77] The interpretation of "legal competence" seems unclear; however it cannot be understood to exclude de facto authority.

Thus one may conclude that the third element which causes criminal responsibility of commanding officer, is the failure to prevent a crime about to be committed by their subordinate or to punish such crime after it has been committed by them.

[77] Internatioal Law Commissionn, Report of the International Law Commission on the work of its forty-eighth session, 1996,p 26

CHAPTER 3

INACTION WHILE UNDER DUTY TO ACT

Neither the statutes of the military tribunals nor the current UN tribunals and the ICC have a prescription on inaction while on duty. However the body of case law of these tribunals and courts could be indicative of an existence of a norm punishing inaction when the accused is under duty to take certain action. This section will proceed to a review of cases before a conclusion is drawn.

3.1 Review of the Jurisprudence of early Tribunals

3.1.1 The Aleksovski Case

Mr Zlatko Aleksovski was warden and exercised control over the Kaonik Prison facilities from 29 January 1993 to May 1993 after which he became Head of the District Heliodrom prison in Mostar.[78] Aleksovski's indictment indicates that detainees under his control were subjected to inhumane treatment, including, excessive and cruel interrogation, physical and psychological harm, forced labour ect...[79]

[78] See ICTY, Zlatko Aleksovski indictement, para 7
[79] Idem, para 31

The Trial Chamber found that even if the chamber did not find that the accused ordered the crimes to be committed, in his capacity as prison warden, he was in charge of organising the body-search of detainees and of supervising them.[80] The Chamber further said that by being present during the mistreatment and not objecting to it, it would be construed as a sign of support and encouragement and thus a substantive contribution to the mistreatment. The Chamber held him responsible for aiding and abetting under article 7(1).[81]

The Trial Chamber further discussed the question of detainees who were taken from the Kaonik prison and were forced to dig trenches and used as human shields. The Trial Chamber found that neither did Mr. Aleksovski order nor plan the trench-digging.[82] However the Trial Chamber found that by his attitude and "his passive presence" when the detainees were taken away to serve as human shields, he manifested his approval of this practice and contributed substantially to the commission of the crime."[83] Thus the Trial Chamber found him criminally responsible for having aided and abetted in the use of detainees as human shields and for the trench digging.

3.1.2 The Essen Lynching Case

In the case known as the Essen Lynching Case in which Captain Erich Heyer and six other were charged before the British Military Court for trial of war criminals, Essen, 18th – 19th and 21st -22nd December, 1945, Private Koener was charged for inactivity while under duty to protect prisoners of war.

Indeed Private Koener was escorting three British Airmen to the Luftwaffe unit for interrogation, when they came under a mob attack and were killed as Private Koener was passively watching. Though his commanding officer had given him order[84] to the escort not to interfere with the crowd could the crowd decide to lynch the three Airmen, however this aspect was never raised during the trial since it could have been considered an illegal order which was not to be taken in to consideration anyway.

[80] See ICTY, Zlatko Aleksovski Trial Judgement, para 87
[81] Idem
[82] Idem, para 123
[83] Idem, para 129
[84] See Law report of trials of war criminals selected and prepared by the United Nations War Crimes Commission,Vol. I, 1949, p 88

During his trial the prosecutor submitted that mere inaction on the part of a spectator is not in itself a crime, however in certain circumstances a person may be under a duty to act. The prosecutor further explained that the escort, as the representative of the Power which had taken the airmen prisoners, had the duty not only to prevent them from escaping but also to protect them and see that they were not molested.

Therefore it was the duty of the escort, who was armed with a revolver, to protect the people in his custody. According to the Prosecutor, Private Koenen failed to do what his duty required him to do. The Court found Private Koener guilty and sentenced him for five years.[85]

3.1.3 The Jaluit Atoll Case

In the Jaluit Atoll Case, Rear-Admiral Nisuke Masuda and four other of the Imperial Japanese Navy were tried by the United States Military Commission, at the United States Air Base, Kwajalein Island, Kwajalein Atoll, Marshall Island, 7th-13th December, 1945.

The accused were charged of killing by shooting unarmed prisoners of war. However Mr. Tasaki who had not participated in the actual killing of the prisoners of war, was charged with the offence of "Liability of custodian who released them to be shot."[86]

Tasaki had been in charge of the prisoners but released them to the executioner to be killed. He was sentenced to ten years of imprisonment after having been found guilty as custodian who releases prisoners to be shot.

[85] Idem, p 90
[86] Idem, pp 71-80

3.2 The Jurisprudence of the current Ad-hoc Tribunals

3.2.1 The Sainovic Case

In the Sainovic case, Dragoljub Ojdanic and Vladmir Lazarevic were found guilty of the crime of forcible transfer of the Kosovo Albanian population and deportation, crimes in which the Trial Chamber found they participated through their acts and omissions.

General Ojdanic was Deputy Chief of the General Staff of the VJ in 1996 later he became the Chief of the General Staff 1998 and Federal Minister of in 2000. Whereas General Lazarevic was Chief of Staff then Commander of the Pristina Corps in 1998, he later was appointed Chief of Staff and then Commander of the Third Army in 2000 before he bacame VJ General Staff as Assistant for Ground Forces where he stayed till 2003.[87]

The Trial Chamber found that General Ojdanic failed to take disciplinary measures against the 3rd Army Commander despite the fact he knew that crimes were being committed at the time its command was under Ojdanic's authority.

The Trial Chamber reasoned that "Ojdanic's failure to take effective measures against Pavkovic provided practical assistance, encouragement, and moral support to members of the VJ who perpetrated crimes in Kosovo, by sustaining the culture of impunity surrounding the forcible displacement of the Kosovo Albanian population, and by allowing the Commander of the 3rd Army to continue to order operations in Kosovo during which the forcible displacement took place."[88]

The Trial Chamber concluded that as Chief of the General Staff, through his acts and omissions, Ojdanic provided practical assistance, encouragement, and moral support to members of the VJ, who were involved in the commission of forcible transfer and deportation to the specific crime sites where it has been found that the VJ participated, and that his conduct had a substantial effect on the commission of these crimes.[89]

---

[87] See ICTY, Milan Milutinovic et al. Indictement, para 5

[88] See ICTY, Milan Milutinovic et al. Trial Judgement, para 627

[89] Idem, para 628

In the same case, the Trial Chamber found that Lazarevic provided practical assistance, encouragement, and moral support to the VJ forces engaging in the deportation and forcible transfer of the Kosovo Albanian population pursuant to Article 7(1) of the Statute for aiding and abetting the crimes of deportation and other inhumane acts as crimes against humanity.

The Trial Chamber said that Lazarevic knew that his failure to take adequate measures to secure the proper investigation of serious crimes committed by the VJ, enabled the forces to continue their campaign of terror, violence, and displacement.[90] The Trial Chamber concluded that these acts and omissions provided a substantial contribution to the commission of the crimes that the Chamber has found to have been committed by VJ members.[91]

Further, the Trial Chamber was of the view that Lazarevic's presence in the field, and his inspection as Commander of the Priština Corps of which units were involved in the commission of crimes against Kosovo Albanians, could be construed to have been designed to improve the morale of these units for the purposes of committing crimes. Thus the Trial Chamber found him having aided and abetted commission of such crimes.

Thus the Trial Chamber established that:

> An accused may aid and abet through an omission, where
> (a) there is a legal duty to act,
> (b) the accused has the ability to act,
> (c) he fails to act either intending the criminal consequences or with awareness and consent that the consequences will ensue, and
> (d) the failure to act results in the commission of the crime.[92]

This position was affirmed by the Appeals Chamber as it stated in the same case that:

> A person may be held criminally responsible for aiding and abetting by omission where he or she fails to discharge a legal

[90] Idem, para 925
[91] Idem, para 926
[92] Idem 620, though the same was refered in para 921

> duty and by this failure assists, encourages or lends moral support to the perpetration of a crime and has a substantial effect on the commission of that crime.[93]

Furthermore, aiding and abetting by omission requires that the accused has the ability to act, that is that the accused had the material capacity to discharge their duties but abstained to do so intending to support the commission of the crime.

Interestingly, General Lazarevic appealed against the Trial Chamber judgment and the Appeals Chamber found that the military justice system's failure to effectively investigate, prosecute, and punish those responsible for committing serious crimes against the civilian population was due to a combination of internal and external factors, of which external factors were beyond Lazarevic's control.[94]

The reasoning of the Appeals Chamber was that considering the situation that prevailed in the field at the time such crimes were committed it would have been unlikely that Lazarevic could have taken measures against the perpetrators, thus his omission might not have reached the required threshold for the Trial Chamber to enter a conviction under this mode of participation.

The Appeals Chamber reversed the judgment of the Trial Chamber in this respect as it said that irrespective of any failure of Lazarevic to take more adequate measures to report, investigate, and initiate disciplinary measures, no reasonable trier of fact could have found beyond reasonable doubt that his omission in this respect had a substantial effect on the commission of the forcible displacement.[95]

Turning to the question of Lazarevic's inspections of and visits to the units in the field, the Appeals Chamber found that there was no evidence indicating that Lazarevic's conduct was construed by the subordinate units as providing encouragement or moral support to the commission of any crime.

---

[93] See ICTY, Sainovic et al. Appeals Judgement, para 1677
[94] Idem, para 1680
[95] Idem, para 1682

The Chamber reversed the judgement of the Trial Chamber in this respect as well as it concluded that Lazarevic's conduct in this respect could therefore not be considered as aiding and abetting the commission of deportation and forcible transfer by the VJ forces.[96]

It should be indicated that in the case as General Ojdanic withdrew his appeal, no further discussion on his mode of participation took place as the Trial Chamber had found him guilty for having participated in the crime of forcible transfer of population through omission.

3.2.2 The Ntagerura Case

In the Ntagerura et al case, the tribunal established that "any omission of this legal duty under Rwandan law, even if proven, does not result in criminal liability under Article 6(1) of the Statute"[97] raising the standard to the requirement of an existence of a legal duty under a rule of criminal law.

The Appeals Chamber recalled that while individual criminal responsibility generally requires the commission of a positive act, this is not an absolute requirement.

In particular, the Appeals Chamber has previously found that "the omission to act where there is a legal duty to act can lead to individual criminal responsibility under Article 7(1) of the Statute". Moreover, the Appeals Chamber has consistently found that, in the circumstances of a given case, the actus reus of aiding and abetting may be perpetrated through an omission.[98]

The same was referred to in the Oric Case as the Appeals Chamber confirmed that omission proper may lead to individual criminal responsibility under Article 7(1) of the Statute where there is a legal duty to act.[99]

---

[96] Idem, para 1689
[97] See ICTR, Andre Ntagerura et al. Appeals Judgement, para 333 in fine
[98] See ICTY, Mrsksic and Sljivancanin Appeals Judgement, para 134
[99] See ICTY, Oric Appeal Judgement, para 43

3.3 Constitutive Elements

3.3.1 The Existence of a Legal Duty to act

As indicated earlier though there is no legal provision on such mode of criminal liability as in international criminal law the idea of punishing individual for inaction is not new. Already article 86 (1) AP I provides that:

The High Contracting Parties and the Parties to the conflict shall repress grave breaches, and take measures necessary to suppress all other breaches, of the Conventions or of this Protocol which result from a failure to act when under a duty to do so.

Thus the first requirement for an omission to be considered as a mode of partipation in a crime is the existence of a legal norm establishing the obligation of the accused to act as a matter of their duty. One could refer to the classic example of prisoners of war who are under the power of the enemy of whom international law has created an obligation to the detaining power to ensure that they are always treated humanely and with dignity.

3.3.2 Actus Reus

Inaction of the aState‘s agent whose duty is the welfare of prisoners of war could lead to their criminal liability in the event that a prisoner of war get mistreated by a third person as the agent refrains to discharge their duty of care. The actus reus of such participation will be constituted of the failure to act, in other words, it consists of the omission to perform their legal duty.

It will be recalled that generally in criminal law, there is a difference between an omission charged against the accused as a way of commision or perpetration of a crime and an omission charged as a mode of participation to a crime. When considered as a way of perpetration, the omission, which is the fact of doing nothing becomes the actus reus of the crime.

3.3.3 Mens Rea

As the present study focusses on the omission as mode of participation, it considers that the actus reus of the crime has been committed by the principal perpetrator when the aider or abettor is charged for participating or facilitating the commission of a crime committed by a different person.

Thus, the mens rea for such participation will be constituted by the fact that the omission intends to encourage or lend moral support to the perpetratration of the actus reus of the crime by the principal offender.

Furthermore, as a general rule the participation of the aider and abettor must have a substantial effect on the perpetrator, and the aider and abettor must know about the commission of the crime which affected his conduct or at least must be aware of some or essential elements of the crime.[100]

In the Blaskic Case, the Appeals Chamber said thatwilful failure to discharge such a duty may incur criminal responsibility pursuant to Article 7(1) of the Statute in the absence of a positive act."[101] This conclusion reasonate in the line of the the Trial Chamber Judgement in the Ntagerura Case in which the Trial Chamber found that "the accused must have had the ability to act."[102]

Thus the omission must result from the decision of the accused not to act for the purposes of facilitating the commission of a crime and not due to other factors as it was proven in theLazarevic case.

[100] See ICTY, Naser Oric Trial Judgement, para 43
[101] See ICTY, Tihomir Blaskic Appeals Judgement, para 663
[102] See ICTR, Andre Ntagerura et al. Trial Judgement, para 659

3.3.4 Complicity by Omission in the Rutaganira Case

In the Rutaganira Case, the Trial Chamber started by establishing the legal ground for the Accused's participation as provided for by the Statutes of the Tribunal. Indeed,as Article 6(1) does not explicitlystipulate for complicityby providing for aiding and abetting.It remains the legal basis for such mode of participation.[103]

The Trial Chamber continues its reasoning by explaining that complicity can occur only by commiting certain acts but also by omission as it has been established by the jurisprudence of the two ad-hoc tribunals before it establishes the requirement ofactus reus and mens rea for such particpation.

3.3.5 Determination on the Actus Reus

According to the reasoning of the trial chamber:

> In determining participation by omission in extermination as a crime against humanity as admitted to by the Accused, the Chamber addressed the following questions:
>
> (i) Did the Accused have authority and did he choose to not exercise it?
>
> (ii) Did the Accused have a moral authority over the principals such as to prevent them from committing the crime and did he choose not to exercise it?
>
> (iii) Was the Accused under a legal duty to act which he failed to fulfill?[104]
>
> (iv) Connection between the perpetration of the crime and participation by aiding and abetting[105]

[103] See ICTR, Vincent Rutaganira Trial Judgement,para 62-63

[104] Idem, para 68

[105] This point was rather brought up in para 84 without having been announced earlier.

This position seems not to resonate in the line of the jurisprudence of the ad-hoc tribunals. Indeed considering the Appeals Chamber position according to which "a person may be held criminally responsible for aiding and abetting by omission where he or she fails to discharge a legal duty and by this failure assists, encourages or lends moral support to the perpetration of a crime and has a substantial effect on the commission of that crime,"[106] one would rather refer to the question which were asked by the Sainovic Trial Chambers, according to which:

> An accused may aid and abet through an omission, where
> (a) there is a legal duty to act,
> (b) the accused has the ability to act,
> (c) he fails to act either intending the criminal consequences or with awareness and consent that the consequences will ensue, and
> (d) the failure to act results in the commission of the crime.[107]

It is therefore unclear whether the question which the Trial Chamber asked could lead to the establishment of the actus reus of an omission as a constitutive element of complicity.

The next section will be focused on their thorough analysis.

3.3.5.1 Establishment of the Authority of the Accused

As indicated above, the Trial Chamber sought to establish the authority that the accused exercised over the principal perpetrators either through the powers vested in him by the statutory provisions or as a moral authority at the time the cirmstances that give rise to theMubuga Commune case.

---

[106] See ICTY, Sainovic et al. Appeal Judgement, para 1677

[107] See ICTY, Sainovic et al., Trial Judgement, para 921; The same was refered to in the ICTR, Jean Mpambara Trial Judgment para 28 amongst other judgments

Indeed, the Trial Chamber was right when it stated that even though the Accused had pleaded guilty it had a duty to satisfy itself that all elements of the crimes were present and that it had to ascertain the form of participation in the perpetration of such crimes.[108]

It is at this point that the wisdom of the Safer HaHinnukh in its commandment 26 could have been beneficial to the Trial Chamber as it provides that: "A person may testify against himself in a court of law, but since he is the accused, ... a second witness is necessary to be able to convict him."[109] The Trial Chamber should have taken upon itself to verify and satisfy itself beyond any reasonable doubt that the guilty plea as negotiated between the Prosecution and the Accused had met the required criteria instead of solely relying to such plea without further inquiries.

It is however doubtful whether the direction taken by the Trial Chamber was to lead to that end. As already discussed, there is a difference between an omission established under article 6(3) providing for command responsibility and an omission established as mode of participation under article 6(1).

When the Chamber is called upon to establish a criminal conduct under the doctrine of command responsibility, the Chamber must first and foremost demonstrate the existence of hierarchy between the accused and the perpetrator, that is, the existence of superior-subordinate relation. This is not the case when the Chamber wants to establish criminal responsibility for aiding and abetting by omission. Indeed establishment of the authority of the accused serves no purpose in this particular case.

Criminal liability will result from the failure to perform a duty which contributed to the commission of the crime. Whether the accused had authority on the perpetrator is not the conclusive question, much more so the source of such authority.

---

[108] See ICTR, Vincent Rutaganira Trial Judgement, para 47

[109] See Sefer HaHinnukh as cited by Chaim Clorfene and Yaakov Rogalsky, The Path of the Righteous Gentile: A Practical Guide to the Seven Laws of Noah, CreateSpace Independent Publishing Platform, 2016, citation 430.

Thus, there might not have been a need for the Chamber to establish that the accused authority derives from a statutory prescription or his moral authority, since the establishment of his participation does not necessarily require that he exercises either legal nor moral authority on the perpetrator; rather, the establishment of his participation starts by determining which duty he failed to accomplish.

In any event the Trial Chamber made reference to Article 37 of the Rwandan law on communal organisation, according to which the position of municipal conseiller communalfor his areaconferred on the Accused authority to chair public meetings in Mubuga Sectorand to note and convey the wishes of the people to the higher authority, namely the Bourgmestre.The Chamber then concluded that such authority implies the power to convene such meetings and to draw up its agendas.[110]

The reasoning of the Chamber was that the Accused had the power to convene a meeting of the inhabitants of the sectorto initiate and conduct discussions on the tragic events that were taking place in his sector, in order to prevent participation in the massacres that occurred at the church, at least, by civilians.[111] The Chamber then concluded that it finds that the Accused's admission that he did not attempt to prevent the attacks on the Tutsi although he was of conseiller communal for the Mubugu Sectoramounted to an implicit admission that he presumably had the power to do so.[112]

The above cited article 37 providing for duties of the at the level of his Sector provides that:

> Le conseiller communal anime, sous la supervision du bourgmestre, les activités de developpement économique, social et culturel de son secteur notamment:
> presider les réunions de la population du secteur
> recueillir et canaliser les aspirations de la population
> entrainer la population dans les actions de développement

[110] See ICTR, Vincent Rutaganira Trial Judgement, para 70
[111] Idem, para 72
[112] Idem, para 73

> collaborer activement avec les agents des services techniques oeuvrant dans la commune pour l'execution du programme gouvernemental.
> Il addresse trimestriellement un rapport de ses activités au bourgmestre.[113]

The above cited provision rather seems to prove the opposite of the presumption of the Trial Chamber. To start with, the meetings of the inhabitants are not meetings at which decisions are made, but are rather held under the supervision of the Bourgmestre who is the official executive officer within the whole commune.

Furthermore, such consultative meetings are designed for the population to voice their views specifically on issues related to their development specifically economic, social and cultural. Most importantly, since these meetings are by no means meetings at which decision are made, the aspirations of the population as expressed from such meetings are then forwarded to the Bourgmestre every three months.

A number of questions could follow the presumption of the power of the Accused by the Trial Chamber such as how does the power to convene a consultative meeting of the inhabitants of a sector with a view of acquiring their opinion translates into authority over the perpetrator of crimes against humanity?

Other than only relying on Accused's admission that he did not attempt to prevent the attacks on the Tutsi although he was Conseiller communalof Mubugu Sector and conclude that such admission amounted to an implicit admission that he presumably had the power to do so, how did the Trial Chamber satisfy itself that indeed the Accused had such powers?

It will be recalled that in the Jean Mpambara case, the Trial Chamber held that: "Although the summaries of the testimony of witnesses contain information which could be characterized as omissions, there is no specification that those omissions are related to a duty to prevent or punish crimes."[114]

[113] See La loi portant sur l'organisation communal du 23 novembre 1963
[114] See ICTR, Jean Mpambara Trial Judgement, para 32

The Trial Chamber reasoned that there was a "failure to distinctly explain that the omissions alleged against the Accused constituted a breach of his duty to prevent or punish the crimes of others."[115] The Trial Chamber decided that "no conviction can fairly be entered against the accused for any alleged default in discharging that duty."[116]

Furthermore it is a general rule that criminal judgments are made on the standard of being beyond reasonable doubt, whereas a judgment based on a mere presumption as stated by the Trial Chamber might be considered as having lowered the required standard in criminal law much more so in international criminal law.

In its reasoning the Trial Chamber relied on the testimony according to which while in office, Mr. Rutaganira had managed to restore security in Mubuga Sectorwhich had experienced growing insecurity caused by bandits and hooligans who used to steal and attack the people.[117]

Such reasoning might be correct except when Mr. Rutaganira restored order and peace in his commune the State machinery was in support of his initiative since all other authorities didn't support the hooliganism which prevailed at that time. The Trial Chamber therefore cannot conclude that because the Conseiller communal was able to stop random bandits, he could have stopped a well organized group of criminals which might have been sponsored by the State[118] to commit international crimes.

Further in an attempt to establish the moral authority of the accused, the Trial Chamber referred to the guilty plea agreement and to the same reasoning of restoration of peace as earlier discussed.

Indeed irrespective of the accused guilty plea, the Trial Chamber was to make its own findings if indeed Mr. Rutaganira was a prominent member and that he was the most important public representative in the Sector; perhaps

[115] Idem, para 34
[116] Idem, para 35
[117] See ICTR, Vincent Rutaganira Trial Judgement, para 71
[118] Indeed para 72 of the judgement suggest that police officers and members of gendarmerie were amongst perpetrators of the attack

most importantly how would that establish the authority he exercised over the perpetrators if that is what the Trial Chamber wanted to establish?

Rather the Trial Chamber found that Mr. Rutaganira exercised authority over the population[119] which should not have been the point, as the focus of the Chamber should have been to demonstrate how the Accused exercised authority over the perpetrators.

Again even if the Conseiller communalcould exercise authority over his population, which was never proven, this does not guarantee he would exercise the same authority over perpetrators amongst which there might have been criminals who originated from other constituencies.

It might be concluded that the Trial Chamber was not obliged to demonstrate the authority exercised by the Accused, over the population, however even its attempt to do so might not have been successful.

3.3.5.2 Establishment of the Legal Duty of the Accused

Certainly the question on establishment of a legal duty on the accused seems to be more relevant to establish the Accused's participation by omission. And to this effect the reasoning of the court was double folded, first it sought to establish such duty from international law provisions, then from domestic law.

A. In International Law

From international law perspective the Trial Chamber found that "ad abundantiam, that international law also places upon a person vested with public authority a duty to act in order to protect human life,"[120] and thus concluded that "as any person, all public authorities have a duty not only to

[119] See ICTR, Vincent Rutaganira Trial Judgement, para 77
[120] Idem, 78

comply with the basic rights of the human person, but also to ensure that these are complied with, which implies a duty to act in order to prevent any violation of such rights."[121]

For the purposes of establishment of the legal duty of the accused to act, the Trial Chamber might have considered identifying precisely which legal norm creates an obligation upon the Accused to adopt a certain conduct, that is to take certain action and demonstrate how the performance of such obligation could have stopped the commission of the crime or at least reduced its impact, or that the omission of the accused contributed to the commission or to the furtherance of such crime.

Thus the Trial Chamber could have gone beyond concluding by implication that there is a duty in international law because it places upon public authority authorities "ad abundatiam," that is, to a great extent without specifying which law it precisely made reference to.

B. In Domestic Law

The Trial Chamber continued its reasoning by looking at the laws applicable in Rwanda as it referred to article 256 of the Rwandan Penal Code according to which:

> Sera puni d'un emprisonnement de deux mois à cinq ans et d'une amende de dix mille francs au maximum, ou de l'une de ces peines seulement :
>
> 1. quiconque pouvant empêcher par son action immédiate, sans risque pour lui ou pour les tiers, soit un fait qualifié crime, soit un délit contre l'intégrité corporelle de la personne, s'abstient volontairement de le faire;
> 2. quiconque s'abstient volontairement de porter à une personne en péril l'assistance que, sans risque pour lui

[121] Idem, 79

ni pour les tiers, il pouvait lui prêter, soit par son action personnelle, soit en provoquant un secours;

3. quiconque, connaissant la preuve de l'innocence d'une personne incarcérée préventivement ou jugée pour crime ou délit, s'abstient volontairement d'en apporter assitôt le témoignage aux autorités de justice ou de police. Echappent à cette disposition le coupable du fait qui motivait la poursuite, ses coauteurs, ses complices, son conjoint, ses parents ou alliés jusqu'au quatrième degré inclusivement. Aucune peine ne sera non plus prononcée contre celui qui, après s'être abstenu, apportera son témoignage tardivement mais spontanément.[122]

This position is perhaps the most striking one. Considering that this article is a legal provision for a crime on its own, it cannot under any circumstances be cited to prove participation in another crime.

Indeed article 256 provides for non assistance à personne en danger which is subject to a different legal regime requiring its own actus reus and mens rea as hereunder discussed.

C. Duty to provide Assistance to People in Danger pursuant to Article 256[123]

As indicated earlier article 256 provides for a "pure crime of omission." Its actus reus is constituted of the existence of a danger, the omission of the accused to assist, the fact that in assisting the person in danger, the accused themselves could not have found themselves in danger. Themens rea of this crime is constituted by the fact that the accused omitted to assist willingly, that is, they decided not to assist as a result of their willingness. They did not want to help.

[122] See Décret-Loi n° 21/77 du 18 août 1977 portant Code Pénal

[123] See ICTR, Vincent Rutaganira Trial Judgement, para 82

In general terms, the crime of omission to assist a person in danger is not an international crime, the statute of the International Criminal Tribunal for Rwanda itself does not have any legal provision with respect to this crime, hence questioning its jurisdiction over the matter, but most importantly it could be erratic to reason that a single element of an actus reus of one crime which is not even fully established could be used to prove participation in a different crime.

D. The Nexus between the Aider and Abettor and the Perpetrator

In seeking to establish the connection between perpetrators of the crime and the Accused, the Trial Chamber found that Mr. Rutaganira "stood a few meters away from the place where the attackers assembled before and after the attacks. Thus, he was in a position to observe them as they assembled near his house and subsequently to know that attacks were being perpetrated on Mubuga church, between 14 and 17 April 1994."[124]

The Trial Chamber then concluded that: "Therefore, the Chamber finds that Vincent Rutaganira participated by omission in extermination as a crime against humanity both before and during the massacre of refugees perpetrated at Mubuga church."[125]

The facts of the case demonstrate that the accused saw the perpetrators assembling. However no indication is made of the accused having heard about the content of the discussion of the alleged attackers about.

For the purposes of satisfying itself beyond any reasonable doubt the Trial Chamber should have found out what was the objective of that assembly as it should have satisfy itself that the group that the Accused saw was indeed the group which committed the alleged crimes at the church.

---

[124] Idem, para 86
[125] Idem, para 87

A number of possibilities could follow a meeting of alleged criminals, a possibility that the group that the accused saw committed a different crime at different place, or altogether failed to agree on the commission of any crime.

Thus, the Trial Chamber needed to satisfy itself beyond a reasonable doubt of the content of the discussion at the said assembly and to establish the nexus between the group that the accused saw and the actual perpetrators of the crimes which were committed at Mabuga church between 14 and 17 April 1994.

E. Substantial Effect on the Commission of the Crime

For the accused to incur criminal liability as aider and abettor their participation needs to have a made a substantial contribution to the commission of the crime. In the instant case the Trial Chamber had to assess the effect that the conduct of the accused had on the perpetrator of the crime which gave rise to this specific case.

Instead the Trial Chamber found that since Rutaganira's intervention had saved some people who had been targeted by attackers in previous instances, then the Trial Chamber inferred that "a similar intervention by the Accused against some civilians who participated in the attacks on Mubuga church would have had the same decisive effect in sparing human lives."[126]

Considering that the Trial Chamber wanted to establish whether the Accused participated to the commission of the crime by having failed to perform his official duty, the Trial Chamber should have referred to cases where the Accused saved human lives precisely by performing his official duty, which is not the case.

126 Idem, para 90

Indeed witnesses who were brought both by the and by the prosecution rather affirmed that the accused saved them by lying about their true identity and not by the exercise of his duty, or at least a combination of the two factors. It therefore cannot be inferred in a different case that the killing in the Mabuga Church could have been prevented if Mr. Rutaganira could have discharged his duty.

Reasoning by inference applies when the sought conclusion is the only possibility and not when such conclusion is of other possibilities. In the case at hand it wasn't established that cases where the Accused intervened, he did so by the virtue of his office, therefore such cases might not be eligible for any reasoning by inference.

Last and certainly not least, for the participation of the accused to have an effect on the perpetrator, the perpetrator must be aware of the assistance of the aider or abettor. Unfortunately the Trial Chamber never made any finding on such an important issue.

The facts of the case are that the Accused saw the perpetrators assembling but it is doubtful if the perpetrators saw him. As it was held in the Blaskic case, "the actus reus of aiding and abetting may be perpetrated through an omission, provided this failure to act had a decisive effect on the commission of the crime.“[127]

This element needed to be established beyond any reasonable doubt. It is fundamental and without a such determination, no conviction can be entered for participation, yet the Trial Chamber made no determination on it.

As per the findings of the Trial Chamber, the chamber was satisfied that "[p]rior to the attack, the Accused had observed the attackers, including the Bourgmestre, armed Hutu civilians, commune policemen and members of the national gendarmerie assembling."[128]

---

[127] See ICTY, Blaskic Trial Judgement, para 284
[128] See ICTR, Vincent Rutaganira Trial Judgement, para 32

Even though the Trial Chamber never made any finding in this respect, one might need to find out to what extend the inaction of the Conseiller could have on the determination of the perpetrator to commit the crime when already the Bourgmester, police officer and gendarmes are already present at the assembling.

Throughout, the reasoning of the Trial Chamber has been that Mr. Rutaganira did nothing when he saw attackers assembling and refrained from exercising either his legal or moral authority; one might ask what authority did a Conseiller have in a meeting attended by the Bourgmestre who is his direct supervisor?

In other words, which specific action could the Accused have taken against a meeting attended by the above indicated authorities to prevent them from committing the alleged crimes?

Thus, the nature of the mode of participation that the accused was convicted for, would have required that at least the Trial Chamber make a determination on the assessment of the effect of the contribution of the Accused, and failure to do so might raise questions on the judgment as a whole.

Considering that the requirement that not only the accused's omission must have substantial effect upon the perpetrator, it also must be to assist, encourage or lend moral support to the perpetrator, and none of these elements was established by the Trial Chamber.

3.3.6 Determination on the Mens Rea

When making a finding on the mens rea, it is required for the Chamber to satisfy itself that the aider and abettor was aware of the crime to be committed by the principal perpetrator or at least its essential elements and he must have known that his omission was to assist the commission of the crime of the principal perpetrator.

The reasoning of the Trial Chamber when establishing how the accused knew about the crime was by imputing such knowledge by virtue of his position as conseiller communal for Mubuga secteur.

Thus the Trial Chamber found that "the Accused must have known about the serious events that were occurring in his secteur and the crimes that were being perpetrated there on a large scale."[129] The Trial Chamber then concluded that: "In the light of the above the Chamber finds that the Accused knew about the general context in which the massacres were being perpetrated at Mubuga church during the relevant period."[130]

It is questionable if the knowledge required in this instance is a general knowledge of status of lawlessness which resulted into commission of crimes at a large scale or a specific knowledge of which crime was to be committed by the group the Accused saw assembling near his residence.

As indicated earlier, other than seeing the Trial Chamber could have found out if the Accused heard the discussion of the meeting and know that such alleged killers were indeed going to commit killings in the Mubuga Church.

The general knowledge of killing at large scale might not meet the required standard to be held accountable for participating to such crime. Indeed the scale of the killing which took place in Mubuga was of such a magnitude that virtually everybody living in that secteur was aware of it.

The chamber might have needed to make a finding on whether the Accused knew specifically of the attack which took place in the Church between 14-17.04.1994 before such attack.

Furthermore the Trial Chamber found that the Accused knew that his omissions would further the commission of the crime. It could have been easier for the Trial Chamber to make such a finding having established specifically the action that the Accused should have taken, that he was able

[129] Idem, para 95
[130] Idem, para 96

to take and thereafter make a finding on whether he knew that by omitting to take such action he furthered the commission of the crime which should have been his intent thus satisfying the subjective element.

As it was held in Blaskic case, in addition to his knowledge the Accused's conduct needs to have intended to provide assistance to the perpetrator.[131] However any finding in this respect could have had upsetting effects on the entire reasoning in the judgement, hence the silence of the Trial Chamber on this element.

[131] See ICTY, Tihomir Blaskic Trial Judgement, para 286

CHAPTER 4
THE GUILTY PLEA

Born in 1944 in Secteur Mubuga, Commune Gashyita, Prefecture of Kibuye in Rwanda. Vincent Rutaganira was Conseiller Communal at the time crimes which gave rise to this case were committed.[132]

By then the Republic of Rwanda was divided in to Prefectures. The Prefect of the Prefecture, was appointed by the President of the Republic and was the highest representative of the executive at provincial level. At a lower level, the Prefecture was divided in to Communes. Each Commune was lead by a Bourgmestre, nominated by the Minister of the Interior and appointed by the President of the Republic.[133]

The Commune was divided into Secteurs whose leaders were directly elected by the population. Elected council at the level of each Secteur formed the council of Commune. When these crimes were committed, Mr. Vincent Rutaganira was serving as member of the council of the Commune Gashyita as he had been elected by the Secteur Mubuga.

[132] See ICTR, Vincent Rutaganira Trial Judgement, paras 4-5
[133] See ICTR, Clement Kayishema et al. First Amended Indictement, p 2.

Mr. Vincent Rutaganira was initially indicted together with Clement Kayishema, Ignace Bagilishema, Charles Sikubwabo, Aloys Ndimbati, Mika Muhimana, Byandikayo, and Obed Ruzindana for various counts. Though, in the indictment of 6th May 1996, the Prosecutor charged Vincent Rutaganira with the following counts:

- Count 1: Conspiracy to commit genocide, under Article 2(3)(a) of the Statute of the Tribunal.
- Count 14: Genocide, under Article 2(3)(a) of the Statute of the Tribunal.
- Count 16: crimes against humanity (extermination), under Article 3(b) of the Statute of the Tribunal,
- Count 17: Crimes against humanity (murder), under Article 3(a) of the Statute of the Tribunal.
- Count 17: Crimes against humanity (other inhumane acts), under Article 3(i) of the Statute of the Tribunal.
- Count 18: Violation of Article 3 common to the Geneva Conventions, under Article 4(a) of the Statute of the Tribunal.
- Count 19: Violation of Additional Protocol II to the Geneva Conventions, under Article 4(a) of the Statute of the Tribunal.

However following his admission of guilt, as part of the guilty plea agreement, the Prosecution made an amendment of the indictment and request the Trial Chamber to acquit him on counts 1, 14, 15, 17, 18 and 19, leaving the only count which remained on the charge list was count 16: Crimes against humanity (extermination) under article 3(b) of the Statute of the Tribunal, of which he pleaded guilty.

4.1 Legal Basis

Though the jurisprudence of early international tribunals is not as rich as the current Ad-hoc Tribunals with respect to guilty pleas, this practice is not a novelty of the ad-hoc tribunal. It goes without saying rather that such practice was borrowed from the adversarial legal system of common law following events related to the aftermath of the WWII.

Indeed, article 24(b) of the Charter of International Military Tribunal provided that: “The Tribunal shall ask each accused whether he pleads "guilty" or "not guilty."” A similar provision is found in article 15(b) of Charter of International Military Tribunal for the Far East according to which: “The Tribunal will ask each accused whether he pleads "guilty" or "not guilty."”

Article 19 of the ICTR Statute providing for the commencement and conduct of trial proceedings, in its paragraph 3 stipulates that: “The Trial Chamber shall read the indictment, satisfy itself that the rights of the accused are respected, confirm that the accused understands the indictment, and instruct the accused to enter a plea. The Trial Chamber shall then set the date for trial.”

The operational provision of the guilty plea at the International Criminal Tribunal for Rwanda is rather Rule 62 of Rules of Procedure and Evidence which provides for initial appearance of accused and plea. According to Rule 62 of the RPE:

> (A) Upon his transfer to the Tribunal, the accused shall be brought before a Trial Chamber or a Judge thereof without delay, and shall be formally charged. The Trial Chamber or the Judge shall:
>
> (iii) Call upon the accused to enter a plea of guilty or not guilty on each count; should the accused fail to do so, enter a plea of not guilty on his behalf;

The same provision in its paragraph continues saying that:

> (B) If an accused pleads guilty in accordance with Rule 62 (A)(v), or requests to change his plea to guilty, the Trial Chamber shall satisfy itself that the guilty plea:
>
> (i) is made freely and voluntarily;
>
> (ii) is an informed plea;
>
> (iii) is unequivocal; and
>
> (iv) is based on sufficient facts for the crime and accused's participation in it, either on the basis of objective indicia or of lack of any material disagreement between the parties about the facts of the case.

4.2 Advantage of the Guilty Plea

In his separate and dissenting opinion of the Appeals Chambers judgment in the Erdemovic case, Judge Cassese summarised various advantages of a guilty plea in the context of international criminal justice. The Erdemovic case was not only the first case in which the Ad-hoc tribunals discussed at length the practice of guilty it contains the richest discussion on the subject.

Thus, from the Tribunal's view point, the guilty plea might prove useful as it spares considerable time to the tribunal, subsequently saving considerable financial resources which could have been allocated to collection of evidence and appearances of witnesses. Considering that international tribunal was sitting remote from the place where crimes have been committed, any appearance of a witness would imply tedious logistical work, not only with respect to their transport and accommodation but also for their safety during and after the trial.

From the accused's view point, as discussed in the Nikolic case: "When an admission of guilt is coupled with a sincere expression of remorse, a significant opportunity for reconciliation may be created."[134]

Indeed through the sincere acknowledgment of their crimes and the recognition of the suffering they have caused to others, a guilty plea may be more meaningful and significant than a finding of guilt by a trial chamber to the victims and survivors.[135]

Thus, as said by the Trial Chamber an admission of guilt from a person perceived as "the enemy" may serve as an opening for dialogue and reconciliation.[136]

However the Plavsic case might have rather proved the opposite. Indeed, after the glamorous celebration of her guilty plea, Mrs Plavsic soon after her release,dramatically revoked her confession as she denied her remorse

[134] See ICTY, Momir Nikolić Trial Judgement, para 72
[135] Idem
[136] Idem

affirming she never felt nor expressed any remorse for the crime she was convicted for. A commendable analysis of Simic written under the eye-catching title "I Would Do the Same Again": In Conversation with Biljana Plavsic,[137] is revealing.

Thus the word of caution of Regina Rauxloh remains relevant as she says that: "The impact of each plea bargain for peace and reconciliation needs to be evaluated individually."[138] However, the contribution of a guilty plea to peace and reconciliation may vary from case to case. A generalized conclusion might need to be avoided.

4.3 Validity of a Guilty Plea

As per Rule 62(B), four elements needs to be satisfied for the validity of a guilty plea, that is that the guilty plea should have been made freely, it result from an informed decision, it should unequivocal and should be based of sufficient facts, as hereunder discussed.

4.3.1 Voluntariness

In their Joint Separate Opinion Judge McDonald and Judge Vohran outlined that for a guilty plea to be considered having been made freely, it must satisfy two following conditions: That is the requirement that the accused be mentally competent to understand the consequences of their guilty plea and that the plea must not have been the result of any threat, coercion or inducement other than the expectation of receiving credit for a guilty plea by way of some reduction of sentence.[139]

[137] See Olivera Simic′, "I Would Do the Same Again": In Conversation With Biljana Plavsic, International Criminal Justice Review, 1-16, Georgia State University, 2018

[138] See Regina E. Rauxloh, Plea bargaining in international criminal justice: Can the International Criminal Court afford to avoid trials? In The Journal of Criminal Justice Research (JCJR) – Vol.1, No 2, 2011, p 6

[139] See ICTY, Erdemovic Trial Judgement, joint separate opinion Judge Mcdonald and Judge Vohran, 10

4.3.2 Inducement

The concept of inducement during plea negotiations might deserve more attention than it has received. There are questions concerning this concept which have remained unanswered. It needs to be pointed out that the process of plea negotiation is not provided for. It is entirely left to concerned parties as no rule governs neither the procedure nor its content.

In many cases, the Prosecution has requested the Accused to plead guilty on a promise to amend the indictment and has dropped some charges as a result of the plea bargaining. This practice has become socommon that it is not considered as an inducement to the Accused. Nevertheless it is worthy asking whether an amendment of the indictment reducing seven charges to one is not an inducement as it was in the case of Mr. Rutaganira.

For instance immediately after her early release, Mrs. Nljana Plavsic clearly contradicted her guilty plea indicated that she pleaded guilty to crimes against humanity, so she could bargain for the other charges.[140] It worth noting that in this case the Prosecutor dropped other charges including genocide, complicity in genocide, and the following crimes against humanity: persecutions, extermination and killing, deportation and inhumane acts.[141] Indeed this amendment attracted serious criticisms of the Prosecution from scholars, victims and even from the Accused herself.

In the Jean Kambanda case, the Accused was moved from the Tribunal Detention Unit to a very luxurious villa with all the advantages that would normally follow all facilities availed to him which he could not access at the detention unit.[142] In the Rutaganira case the negotiations included the place where he was to serve the sentence.[143]

---

[140] See Olivera Simic´, "I Would Do the Same Again": In Conversation With Biljana Plavsic, International Criminal Justice Review, 1-16, Georgia State University, 2018, p 7

[141] See ICTY, Biljana Plavsic Trial Judgement, para 2

[142] See ICTR, Jean Kambanda Appeal Judgement, para 35

[143] See ICTR, Memoire conjoint entre Vincent Rutaganira et le bureau du Procureur prealable au prononce de la sentence devant la chamber de premiere instance III du Tribunal Penal International pour le Rwanda, para 43

In reality the place of the detention might be a non negligible factor if one considers the huge difference that exists say, between African prisons and European prisons where in one case prisoners are suffocated due to lack of basic facilities including toilet facilities, to European prisons with facilities non affordable to a common resident including sports, sauna, even room massage.

Though the Tribunals have always considered themselves as not bound by the recommendations of the Prosecution with respect to sentencing, the practice rather confirms that when sentencing, the Chambers has taken into consideration such recommendations. It is at this point that one may ask if a bargain on these above factors do not constitute enough incentive to induce the accused to plead guilty?

4.3.3 The Threat

The Cambridge dictionary defines a threat as a suggestion that something unpleasant or violent will happen, especially if a particular action or order is not followed.[144]

The same concept could be understood in the sense of intimidation which is understood as the fact of threatening someone, usually in order to persuade them to do something that you want them to do.

During the Status Conference of 10.07.2004, the Prosecution indicated that "all cases where it is not the highest responsibility must be cases where the Prosecutor considers Rule 11 bis."[145] Rule 11 bis provides for the referral of the indictment to a national jurisdiction, of which in the present case the national jurisdiction was none other than Rwanda.

Considering how the Rwandan justice system worked in the 1994 Aftermath Crisis, forinstance,the International Committee of the Red Cross, which was monitoring conditions in 135 detention facilities in Rwanda, reported how prisons were overcrowded.

---

[144] See https://dictionary.cambridge.org/us/dictionary/english/threat last consulted on 05.08.2019
[145] See ICTR, Vincent Rutaganira Transcript Status Conference 17.09.2004, p 4

In some prisons, four inmates occupied every single square metre of floor space in the open courtyards and six are squeezed into every square metre in the dormitory buildings that surround the courtyards.

Perhaps the most shocking event occurred on March 17, 1995, when soldiers at the Muhima Brigade forced more than sixty persons into a room far too small to accommodate them. During the night they begged to have the door opened because some were dying for lack of oxygen. The guards refused to open the room until the next morning, at which time twenty-two people had suffocated.[146]

Multiple reports by different human rights organisation accused the Rwandan government of summary executions.[147] Thus, a country that never let its prisoners have oxygen to breath cannot be expected to hold fair and impartial trials. Furthermore, Human Rights Watch reported once that: "Virtually, all persons detained have been arrested on the basis of denunciation alone rather than as the result of a criminal investigation."[148]

The same report says that: "The shortage of staff for hearing the enormous number of cases has meant that the vast majority of persons now jailed in Rwanda have been detained without due process."[149]

In the case at hand, could the suggestion of the referral of the Rutaganira case had implication in the decision of the defence to opt for a guilty plea instead of relying on the safeguard measures provided for under Rule 11bis? If this question is answered in positive could such possibility be considered a threat?

---

[146] See Human Rights Watch, Rwanda: The Crisis Continues, Vol. 7, No 1, April 1995, pp 3-4

[147] See Human Rights Watch and the International Federation of Human Rights Leagues (FIDH) on their report of the 20th August 1997 on Massacre of Civilians by Rwandan Soldiers and Armed Insurgents

[148] See Human Rights Watch, Rwanda: The Crisis Continues, Vol. 7, No 1, April 1995, p 5

[149] Id.,

4.3.4 An Informed Decision

In the Plavsic case, the guilty plea agreement co-signed by the Prosecution and the indicated that:

> By pleading guilty, Biljana Plavsic understands that she will be giving up the following rights:
> (a) The rights to plead not guilty and require the Prosecution to prove the charges in the Indictment beyond a reasonable doubt at a fair and impartial public trial;
> (b) The right to prepare and put forward a defence to the charge at such public trial
> (c) ...
> (d) ...
> (e) The right to examine at her trial, or have examined, the witness against her and to obtain the attendance and examination of witnesses against her and to obtain the attendance and examination of witness on her behalf at a trial under the same condition as witnesses against her.[150]

However as indicated by Simic, "She often complained about not having opportunity to speak and present her viewpoints during her time in the courtroom."[151] This raises a query whether by agreeing that she had given up her right to examination of witness she understood what that entailed.

The earlier discussed requirement of mental capacity which would rather refer to the sanity of mind of which enable the accused take responsibility of their decision should not be confused with the requirement of the understanding of the legal consequence required to a guilty plea to be considered an informed one. The former requirement refers to a psychological capacity the later refers to a legal competence. But most importantly, the first does not necessarily imply the second.

[150] See ICTY, Biljana Plavsic agreement plea, para 10
[151] Olivera Simic´, "I Would Do the Same Again": In Conversation With Biljana Plavsic, International Criminal Justice Review, 1-16, Georgia State University, 2018, p5

The Erdemovic case, provides an illustration of such situation whereby the Trial Chamber received a report of the commission of medical expert affirming that the Accused was in condition sufficient for him to stand the trial,[152] however the Appeals Chamber found that he and probably his lawyer failed to understand the legal consequence of a guilty plea thus considering it uninformed.

As explained in the Joint Separate Opinion of Judge McDonald and Judge Vohrah, in the Erdemovic case, after entering a guilty plea the is not expected to submit arguments defeating the guilty plea by advancing argument contradicting either the admission of guilt or the criminal responsibility of the accused which is the very object of the guilty plea.[153]

4.4 The Rutaganira Guilty Plea

As the guilty plea agreed between the Prosecution and the stipulate that:

> L'accusé Vincent RUTAGANIRA et le Procureur ont conclu un accord le 7 décembre 2004 aux fins que l'accusé plaide coupable, en tant que complice pour le chef d'extermination constitutif du crime contre l'humanité en vertu de l'article 3(b) du statut du Tribunal tel qu'inciminé dans le chef d'accusation 16 de l'acte d'accusation.[154]

Such concession would mean that the Accused has forfeited his right to the trial, and he has accepted his criminal responsibility as having participated to in the commission of the crime as an accomplice.

---

[152] See ICTY, Drazen Erdemovic Trial Judgement, para 8

[153] See ICTY, Drazen Erdemovic Trial Judgement, Joint Separate Opinion of Judge McDonald and Judge Vohrah, para16

[154] See ICTR, Memoire conjoint entre Vincent Rutaganira et le bureau du Procureur prealable au prononce de la sentence devant la chamber de premiere instance III du Tribunal Penal International pour le Rwanda, para 8

When discussing whether the decision to plead guilty is an informed decision, the legal requirement for the validation of the guilty plea with respect to this element is that the should not put forth any argument which aims at defeating the criminal responsibility of the accused either by denied the perpetration or the participation of the accused to the crime as a matter of law.

In other words, since the guilty plea would mean acceptance that the Accused has indeed committed the crime, they cannot plead guilty, that is to accept their criminality; to defend themselves would automatically invalidate the guilty plea. This is what justifies the shortening of the procedure since there would not be any trial "stricto senso." After the admission of guilt, submissions are made and the proceedings moves to sentencing!

In legal terms, whereas mitigating circumstances are allowed before sentencing following a guilty plea, anything in which aims at grounds excluding the criminal responsibility of the Accused, defeats the guilty plea. It would invalidate the guilty plea in the sense that defence does not accept the legal responsibility of the Accused.

In the Rutaganira case, the defence submitted that:

> In its deliberations the Chamber should consider the different legislation regarding non-assistance to persons in danger. It should also consider Article 31 of the statute of the International Criminal Court. Each of those legislations considers a person guilty when that person fails to intervene, when he is in a position to do so without danger to himself. That means that the absolute danger is justification, absolute justification which excludes any guilt whatsoever.[155]

[155] See ICTR, Vincent Rutaganira Transcript Status Conference 8.12.2004, pp 32-33

Considering that grounds excluding criminal responsibility provide a legal ground to discharge the accused from their criminal responsibility which contradict the very reason of a guilty plea.

Though the substance of the argument would have been subject to a legal discussion, as a matter of formality, by submitting an argument justifying the behaviour of the Accused in terms of exclusion of guilt, the Trial Chamber might have considered further inquiry before it declared Accused guilty!

4.4.1 Unequivocal Plea

In simple terms, if a guilty plea is considered informed when the defence does not submit a legal objection which could exclude criminal responsibility of the accused, an unequivocal plea is rather a plea which does not contain any factual ground of defence which tends to justify the Accused.

In this case the defence will refrain from making factual allegations which are disculpatory in nature. In theory any description of facts which aims at proving the innocence of the accused would defeat the guilty plea, which indeed alters the presumption of innocence.

In the Rutaganira Case, during the sentencing trial, the Prosecution went on with the following description of facts:

> The fact that prior to the attack at Mubuga church, Mr. Rutaganira actually saw the assailants who later attacked that church. He saw them gather in front of his residence, and, as I said earlier, Mr. Rutaganira's residence was located approximately 500 metres from the said church. Now, the assailants who gathered outside Mr. Rutaganira's residence consisted of other local authorities like himself. They included Bourgmestre Charles Sikubwabo, and

> Hutu civilians, communal policemen, and even members of the Nationale Gendarmerie. We consider as particularly aggravating, Your Honour, the fact that Mr. Rutaganira was aware, at minimum, that the presence of all these local authorities in and around the area of Mubuga church would have had an encouraging effect on the assailants and would have given those assailants the distinct impression that the killing of Tutsi civilians who were gathered 500 metres away was something that was endorsed by the local authorities, including himself. We consider particularly aggravating the fact that Mr. Rutaganira himself was aware that these people gathered in the church were subsequently attacked by those assailants.[156]

When Mr Rutaganira was called upon to for his statement his description of facts was as follow:

> I wish to speak to you a little about what happened at the Mubuga church. The church was being guarded by gendarmes 24 hours out of 24 hours from the 10th April to the 18th April 1994, which was the last day of the massacre. These gendarmes were brought there by Préfet Clement Kayishema so that they could ensure the security of the refugees there and they had the right to -- he had the right to stop those criminals and to arrest them. They were -- the gendarmes were the first to kill the refugees instead of protecting them.[157]

A certain contradiction could be seen from these two statements. As the Prosecution alleges that the Accused saw the assailants who attacked the church, Mr. Rutaganira version of facts is that the church was attacked first by the gendarmes who were guarding the place.

---

[156] See ICTR, Vincent Rutaganira Sentencing Trial Transcript, p. 6
[157] Idem, p. 39

Furthermore, whereas the defence concedes that Vincent Rutaganira, admits that despite the fact that he was conseiller of Mubuga secteur, he failed to protect the Tutsis who had sought refuge at Mubuga church in Mubuga secteur, between the 8th and the 15th of April 1994.

The guilty plea agreement rather highlights that:

> En outre il est constant qu'en tant que conseiller de secteur, il n'avait aucune autorité sure les forces de l'ordre, tandisque lui-meme était soumis a l'autorité du Bourgmstre.[158]

On contrary the Trial Chamber affirmed that: "Despite his position and of his having knowledge of the above-mentioned events, the Accused failed to act to protect the Tutsi, either before or after the massacres."[159] Indeed that the Guilty Plea Agreement itself states that the Accused had no authority over the principal perpetrators; it would have been appropriate for the Trial Chamber to request for clarification since these statements might defeat the purpose of the guilty plea.

If it was confirmed that the Accused had no authority it would mean that he could not be found guilty since his failure to act did not result from his intention to assist the commission of the crime but rather resulted from his lack of authority for which he might not necessarily be found guilty.

Indeed if it was to be confirmed rather that the crimes were committed by the gendarmes as submitted by the Accused, the Trial Chamber should not had entered a guilty plea based on the fact that the Accused saw people assembling before and after commiting the cimes.

At minimum the Trial Chamber was under duty to clarify facts and circumstances of the commission of the crimes. Since there cannot be any link

---

[158] See ICTR, Memoire conjoint entre Vincent Rutaganira et le bureau du Procureur prealable au prononce de la sentence devant la chamber de premiere instance III du Tribunal Penal International pour le Rwanda, para 39

[159] See ICTR, Vincent Rutaganira Trial Judgement, para 33

between the alleged criminals who were seen by the Accused and the crimes by the gendarmes who might have not been part of the meeting from which criminal liability if the Accused is established.

In the Babic case, after a thorough examination of the guilty plea, the Trial Chamber found that the statement of facts failed to accurately give the description of the suggested legal characterisation and it subsequently did not accept the guilty plea agreement in which the Accused was considered aider and abettor but later accepted the guilty plea in which the Accused accepted to plead guilty as co-perpetrator.[160]

4.4.2. Sufficient Incriminating Facts

The last requirement for the validation of the guilty plea is that it must be based on sufficient facts for the crime and accused's participation in it. In other words, there must be sufficient factual basis for the crime and the accused's participation to such crime. This is proven either on the basis of independent indicia or on lack of any material disagreement between the parties about the facts of the case.[161]

In the Deronjic case, the Accused had pleaded, however the Trial Chamber did find discrepancies between the amended indictment and the agreed facts; it thus invited parties to provide further clarification as it didn't enter a finding of guilt until after it had had the benefit of reviewing other evidence admitted, and after hearing the of Accused's witness testimony.[162]

The Trial Chamber had also accepted the Prosecution witness statement, the Defence witness statement and the transcript of the Accused's testimony in another case were ordered to be produced by the prosecution and were

[160] See ICTY, Milan Babic Appeals Judgement, para 9
[161] See ICTY, Rules of Procedure and Evidence, Rule 62bis
[162] See ICTY, Miroslav Deronjic Trial Judgement, para 29

accepted as part of evidence at the sentencing hearing.[163] The Trial Chamber entered the guilty plea after it had found that the discrepancies had been resolved and that there existed sufficient factual basis for the guilty plea under Rule 62bis of the Rules [164]

Thus in the Babic case the Appeals Chamber highlighted that after the parties have entered into negotiations and had agreed on the facts underlying the charges to which the accused will plead, the parties might also submit, "any relevant information that may assist the Trial Chamber in determining an appropriate sentence".[165]

The Appeals Chamber further noted that the Trial Chamber would exercise its discretion in determining the sentences on the basis of the facts agreed upon by the parties as well as the additional information provided by the parties, including those facts presented during the sentencing hearing.[166]

Thus it could be safely concluded that the Trial Chamber might not need to make further findings on facts particularly when such facts are not disputed by the parties and there is not objective indicia of disagreement. It follows that if there were disputed facts or an indicia thereof, the court might either seek more information before it enters the guilty plea or altogether does not enter a guilty plea.

However since the validation of the guilty plea depends on the decision of the Trial Chamber, it is therefore left to the Trial Chamber to assess whether the factual basis for the crime had sufficiently been established before it proceeds with the sentencing. The law does not impose any specific procedure to the Trial Chamber in this respect.

[163] Idem, para 30
[164] See ICTY, Miroslav Deronjic Appeals Judgement, para 3
[165] See ICTY, Milan Babic Appeals Judgement, para 18
[166] Idem, para 18

4.4.3 The Procedure

The consequence of a guilty plea is that the accused has accepted their criminal conduct and have waived their right to be tried for the counts they have been charged with in the indictment. This simplifies the procedure since the Trial Chamber is rather called upon to shorten the process and proceed with what could have been the step after the judgment, the sentencing.

Rule 62bis of the Rules, not only provides for the substantive law for validation of the guilty plea but it also provides albeit in short for the procedure. Accordingly:

> Upon his transfer to the Tribunal, the accused shall be brought before a Trial Chamber or a Judge thereof without delay, and shall be formally charged. The Trial Chamber or the Judge shall:
>
> ...
>
> (iii) Call upon the accused to enter a plea of guilty or not guilty on each count; should the accused fail to do so, enter a plea of not guilty on his behalf;
>
> ...
>
> (v) In case of a plea of guilty:
>
> (a) if before a Judge, refer the plea to the Trial Chamber so that it may act in accordance with Rule 62 (B); or
>
> (b) if before a Trial Chamber, act in accordance with Rule 62 (B).

As a matter of compliance with fair trial requirement, soon after the accused is at the disposal of the Tribunal either by surrender or by arrest, they must be formally charged without delay. That is the initial hearing where the accused is officially informed by the Tribunal of the charges against them in a language that they understand. This procedure would usually take place before a single judge.

In the Rutaganira case, the Accused voluntarily surrendered to the tribunal on 04.03.2002, the first hearing took place on 07.03.2002 before the single Judge Andrésia Vaz. However on this date both parties the Prosecution and the Defence requested for the adjournment of the initial hearing. It was adjourned to 23.03.2002.

It is in its initial hearing of the 23.03.2002 that charges were read to Mr. Rutaganira in Kinyarwanda as he had requested, in accordance with the law. At this hearing the Accused pleaded not guilty to all charges against him. Having taken note of the Accused's declaration the Single Judge closed the session after having reminded the parties of the next trial procedure considering that the Accused had pleaded not guilty.

On 1.08.2004 the Defence filed a motion to set a date for trial and to seek release pending trial under rule 73 of the Rules of Procedure and Evidence. After having explained that the Accused considered that neither his right to a date for the commencement of trial following his initial appearance nor his right to be tried within a reasonable time had been complied with and that he was justified in requesting that the date for his trial be set without delay, the defence requested the Trial Chamber to:

> CONFIRM to the that it is ready to commence the trial of the Accused on the basis of the current Indictment;
> ORDER the Registry to set a date for commencement of the Accused's trial or alternatively to set a date for a status conference, pursuant to Rule 65 bis of the Rules
> Should the Tribunal fail to set a date for commencement of trial, ORDER the provisional release of the Accused pursuant to Rule 65(A) of the Rules.[167]

Rule 65(A) provides that: "Once detained, an accused may not be provisionally released except upon an order of a Trial Chamber. Once detained, an accused may not be provisionally released except upon an order of a Trial Chamber."

167 See ICTR, Vincent Rutaganira, Motion to set a date for trial and to seek release pending trial, under ruel 73 of the Rules of procedure and Evidence, pp 4-5

On the 16.08.2004, the Prosecution responded that the Trial Chamber could set the Status Conference as provided for under Rule 65bis (A) of the Rules at which issues pertaining to provisional release, trial readiness and status of the case would be explored. Further the Prosecution requested that save for the relief for a Status Conference the rest of relief sought the defence should be dismissed.[168]

The above referred to Rule 65bis (A) provides that: "A status conference may be convened by a Trial Chamber or a Judge thereof. Its purpose is to organize exchanges between the parties so as to ensure expeditious trial proceedings."

On the 03.09.2004 the Trial Chamber issued a decision to the Defence application rejected the request for a date of commencement of the trial as well as the request for the provisional release of the Accused, however the Trial Chamber ordered the parties to appear for the Status Conference on the 17.09.2004.[169]

At the Status Conference of 17.09.2004, the Prosecution opened the floor by making reference to an undisclosed letter which had been given to the Defence on the Prosecution's policy. The prosecution explained that it had made a suggestion to the Defence which is subject of negotiations as to how the trial could continue.

Considering that such suggestion could require the Defence to take time with the Accused before any decision is made, and since the suggestion could necessitate a lot of correspondence between the Office of the Prosecutor and the Defence, the Prosecutor requested that a further Status Conference be scheduled in December.[170]

---

168 See ICTR, Vincent Ruataganira, Prosecutor's response to the defense motion for setting of a trial date of Status Conference or alternatively provisional release p 3

169 See ICTR, Vincent Ruataganira, Decision relative a la requite aux fins de fixation de la date d'ouverture du proces ou alternativement de la convocation d'une conference de mise en etat et de sa mise en liberte proviso ire, p 4

170 See ICTR, Vincent Rutaganira Status Conference of 17.09.2004, Tanscript p 2

In response the Defence acknowledged having received the Prosecution's letter and suggested that the next Status Conference is held on 08.12.2004, however the Defence still requested that apart from the said letter that the prosecution disclose what was its plan as far as the Rutaganira case is concerned, and if it was ready to start the trial, if so at what date?[171]

The prosecution responded that the matter was subject to policy consideration where cases in which the Accused who do not bear the highest responsibility might be subjected to Rule 11bis of the Rules[172] which provides for the referral of cases to national jurisdiction as discussed bellow.

4.4.4 Rule 11bis of the Rules

According to Rule 11bis (A) of the Rules:

> If an indictment has been confirmed, whether or not the accused is in the custody of the Tribunal, the President may designate a Trial Chamber for the purpose of referring a case to the authorities of any State that is willing to prosecute the accused in its own courts, so that the authorities of the State concerned should forthwith refer the case to the appropriate court for trial within that State.

The Prosecutions had started considering referral of some casesto Rwanda as part of its completion strategy since late 2003.[173] The process would materialize in 2007 with a total of five[174] applications for referral to Rwanda which were made submitted to the Referral Chamber in the second half of the year 2007.

171 Idem, p 3
172 Idem, p 4
173 See ICTR, OTP, Complementarity in action: Lessons learned from the ICTR Prosecutor's referral of international criminal cases to national jurisdictions for trial, 2015, p 14
174 These cases include, Prosecutor v. Fulgence Kayishema, Case No. ICTR-2001-67-I, Prosecutor v. Gaspard Kanyarukiga, Case No. ICTR-2002-78-I, Prosecutor v. Yussuf Munyakazi, Case No. ICTR-97-36-I, 7 September 2007, Prosecutor v. Ildephonse Hategekimana, Case No. ICTR-00-55-I, Prosecutor v. Jean-Baptiste Gatete, Case No. ICTR-2000-61-I, 28 November 2007.

Though so far none of such application has been successful considering that the implementation of a referral is conditioned by Rule 11bis (C) of the Rules according to which the Trial Chamber must:

(i) [S]atisfy itself that it is appropriate in the circumstances for the courts of the State concerned to exercise jurisdiction over the accused, and

(ii) [S]atisfy itself that the accused will receive a fair trial with due process in the courts of the State concerned.

Subsequently a second round of the Prosecutor's application for referral was launched in 2010 of which some cases were successfully referred to Rwanda including the Uwikindi and Munyagishari cases.

In the Rutaganira Case, indications that the Prosecution was considering the application of Rules 11bis of the Rules, might have weighted into the considerations of negotiations of a guilty plea of which the defence would be part of or rely on the rejection of such application by the Referral Chamber.

The length of the process of referral proceedings might also have been another factor which the Defence might have taken into consideration, in average the process of referral took four year for the Appeals Chamber to reject first round of referral applications, as Rutaganira had been already in custody for two years, could he have opted to rely on Rule 11bis (c) at the time of the end of the referral proceedings he would have been in the UN custody for six years, before he restarted the trial proceeding.

A consideration of a guilty plea for a crime which is punishable for six years of imprisonment at the end of which the Accused will be released might have been a factor to take into consideration.

Thus, the Status Conference of 17.09. 2004 was adjourned after the parties had agreed to allow themselves the needed time for further negotiations.

The second Status Conference took place on 08.12.2004 and was held in two appearances; in its first appearance, the parties informed the Chamber that they had reached an agreement on a guilty plea.

The Prosecution informed the Trial Chamber that in return for the guilty plea, the Prosecutor had planned to ask the Trial Chamber to dismiss the remainder of the charges in the indictment, and those charges were set out in Count number 1, Count number 14, Counts number 15, 17, 18, and 19.[175]

The Defencein its turn confirmed the submission of the Prosecution and requested that a further appearance is immediately held to enable the Accused to enter a guilty plea.

In his further appearance on 08.12.2004, the Accused was brought before the Trial Chamber and entered a guilty plea for count 16 which charged him for crimes against humanity,(extermination) a violation of Article 3 of the Tribunal statute. Mr Rutaganira entered a guilty plea saying: "That is where I plead guilty in aiding and abetting by way of omission."[176]

As per Rule 62 (B) of the Rules requiring the Trial Chamber to satisfy itself of the conditions of validity of a guilty plea. The Trial Chamber proceeded by putting questions to the Accused to ascertain his plea was entered willingly, knowingly, and without any coercion or threat or promise.

It remains questionable whether a Trial Chamber would find out whether a guilty plea is unequivocal simply by asking the Accused whether they understand the nature of charges made against them, as well as the consequences of their guilty plea. Neither can the Trial Chamber ascertain that that a guilty plea is an informed plea simply by asking the Accused whether their entered a guilty plea knowingly.

175 See ICTR, Vincent Rutaganira Status Conference of 08.12.2004, Tanscript p2
176 Idem p6

Nevertheless Rule 62 (B) in fine provides that after entering a finding of guilt, the Trial Chamber instructs the Registrar to set a date for the sentencing hearing. The Trial Chamber retired at this point for a brief suspension of the hearing;by the time it resumed the hearing, the Trial Chamber declared the guilty plea valid and directed the registry to set the date of 17.01.2005 for the trial.

> It needs to be stressed that article 19 of the ICTR Statute providing for commencement and conduct of trial proceedings in its paragraph 3 stipulates that:
>
> > The Trial Chamber shall read the indictment, satisfy itself that the rights of the accused are respected, confirm that the accused understands the indictment, and instruct the accused to enter a plea. The Trial Chamber shall then set the date for trial.

This provision which might have been inspired by the inquisitorial legal system of civil law could have been drafted without further consideration of a guilty plea and its implication on the trial procedure. Thanks to Rule 6, it rather remain the guiding rule on the procedure of trial in case of a guilty.

The reasoning in case of a plea being that since the accused had accepted his guilt he is no longer considered innocent until proven guilty. Thus the trial is shortened as there will not be a justification of going through a full trial since the burden of proof upon the Prosecution is substantially lessened by such guilty plea who would not be required to prove his case through the normal lengthy and costly judicial procedure of adducing evidence, bringing witnesses and cross examining to prove facts which are not contested by the accused. Therefore after the Accused has entered a guilty plea, no Trial is expected to take place rather a sentencing hearing.

4.5. The Sentencing Hearing

The difference from the trial and a sentencing hearing is that the accused does not need to defend themselves thus there is no room for dispute of facts or the participation of the accused at this point. However mitigating and/or aggravating circumstances are accepted at this point as they rather pertain to the determination of the sentence but not to the establishment of criminality of the accused.

Thus Rule 100(A) of the Rules providing for the sentencing procedure for a guilty plea stipulates that; "If the Trial Chamber convicts the accused on a guilty plea, the Prosecutor and the Defence may submit any relevant information that may assist the Trial Chamber in determining an appropriate sentence."

It is in the same vein that Rule 101(B) of the Rules provides that:

> In determining the sentence, the Trial Chamber shall take into account the factors mentioned in Article 23 (2) of the Statute, as well as such factors as:
> (i) Any aggravating circumstances;
> (ii) Any mitigating circumstances including the substantial cooperation with the Prosecutor by the convicted person before or after conviction;
> (iii) The general practice regarding prison sentences in the courts of Rwanda;
> (iv) The extent to which any penalty imposed by a court of any State on the convicted person for the same act has already been served, as referred to in Article 9 (3) of the Statute.

Contrary to the Rules of Procedure and Evidence of the ICC[177] the Rules of the ICTR and the Statute do not indicate which elements should be considered as mitigating or aggravating circumstances this lack of legal precision has left parties to make reference to international jurisprudence and at times to national practice.

4.5.1 The Prosecution's Submission

During the sentencing hearingin the Rutaganira Case, the Prosecution started by pleading aggravating circumstances before they pleaded mitigating circumstances. The Prosecution considered particularly aggravating the fact that the accused was Conseiller.[178] However this argument isn't well settled. If one considers the element as part of the constitutive element of the crime it therefore cannot be considered part of the crime and at the same time an aggravating circumstance.

The same critique might apply to the Accused's passiveness as aggravating circumstance, indeed the prosecution argued that the fact that the presence of local authorities would have an encouraging effect on assailants.[179] Although this is precisely the element which was considered for the determination of the Accused's participation and cannot be brought back as an aggravating circumstance.

[177] Rule 145(2) of the ICC Rules provides that: "In addition to the factors mentioned above, the Court shall take into account, as appropriate:
(a) Mitigating circumstances such as:
(i)The circumstances falling short of constituting grounds for exclusion of criminal responsibility, such as substantially diminished mental capacity or duress;
(ii) The convicted person's conduct after the act, including any efforts by the person to compensate the victims and any cooperation with the Court;
(b) As aggravating circumstances:
(i) Any relevant prior criminal convictions for crimes under the jurisdiction of the Court or of a similar nature;
(ii) Abuse of power or official capacity;
(iii) Commission of the crime where the victim is particularly defenseless;
(iv) Commission of the crime with particular cruelty or where there were multiple victims;
(v) Commission of the crime for any motive involving discrimination on any of the grounds referred to in article 21, paragraph 3;
(vi) Other circumstances which, although not enumerated above, by virtue of their nature are similar to those mentioned.

[178] See ICTR, Vincent Rutaganira Setencing Hearing of 17.01.2005, Tanscript p 6

[179] Idem, p 6

The Prosecution further submitted what it considered mitigating circumstances including the fact that the Accused had presented remorse during his guilty plea after having voluntarily surrendered himself to the Tribunal.[180]

The Prosecution highlighted the fact that previous to the events which occurred in 1994, Mr. Rutaganira was a person of good character having no history of extremism,[181] a personal element relevant to the sentencing process.

After having acknowledged not having addressed the aspect regarding the sentencing practice in Rwanda as provided for by Rule 101(B)(iii) of the Rules, and indeed the Prosecution is not under obligation to address all aspects detailed under Rule (B) of the rules. These elements are provided on case by case basis according to the relevance of available elements in a given cas.

In conclusion, the Prosecution recommended a term of imprisonment between six to eight years with credit for the period already served on remand. The Prosecution ended its submission recommending that the Accused be allowed to serve his sentence in prison facility either in Europe or in the kingdom of Swaziland.[182]

4.5.2 The Defence Submission

During the sentencing hearing, the Defence submitted mainly mitigating circumstances. The Defence started by calling witnesses who testified on the personal character[183] of the accused the defence articulated that the Accused had no previous criminal record, then submitted a health certificate proving his health condition.[184] The Defence also pleaded the advance age of the accused, his family status and his good conduct during the time of his detention.[185] Further the Defence pleaded that the Accused accepted his guilt.

---

[180] Idem, p 7
[181] Idem
[182] Idem, p 8
[183] Idem, p 9
[184] Idem, p 13
[185] Idem, p 29

Interestingly during the sentencing hearing the defencesubmitted that "the crime for which Vincent Rutaganira is pleading guilty is based on the offence of omitting to provide assistance to a person in danger, something which is also referred to, non-assistance to a person in danger, which exists in some national codes.[186]

It's not clear what motivated the Defence to make such submission at the sentencing hearing since it is not designed to establish the criminal conduct of the accused but perhaps it would be more questionable to raise such point for reasons discussed under the constitutive elements of a punishable omission in international law.

The Defence further argued the state of necessity but not as a reason for total exemption of the Accused but as a mitigating element, making reference to the landmark Erdomovic case,[187] arguing how the Accused had no authority over the forces of the law and how he was subjected to the authority of the Bourgmestre.

In conclusion the Defence reviewed how omissions are sanctioned in some domestic legislations and making reference to sentencing practice omission in Rwanda courts which punishes omission for five years imprisonment maximum and a maximum fine of 10 000 Rwandan francs.[188]

Before the hearing was adjourned the Trial Chamber called upon the Accused who made his final statement that as it has already been discussed. Thus making an end to his trial as the Trial Chamber was convened on Monday 14.03.2005 to deliver its judgment.

[186] Idem, p 28
[187] Idem, p 35
[188] Idem, p 35

CHAPTER 5

CRIMES AGAINST HUMANITY

5.1 Historical Development

Man's inhumanity against another man is not a recent phenomenon. History has no shortage of such examples, for instance Felix Reichen[189] in his study of the killing of the native Amerindians upon arrival of Europeans around the 18th century, the same having been discussed by David Svaldi among others.[190] Certainly the American case is but an example of what happened elsewhere, indeed Africans might have experienced the same often, including during the time of slavery with the contact of Arabs slave traders but also at the time of colonialism.

Nevertheless the concept of crimes against humanity took the international stage with killings of Armenians in the Ottoman Empire, though as clearly explained by Professor Cassese, the expression crime against humanity was not in the original proposal emanating from Russia which had suggested crime against Christianity and civilisation.

It was due to the fact that France feared that Muslim population under French and British colonies proposed crimes against humanity in replacement of the earlier suggested crime against Christianity and civilisation, and such proposal was adopted.[191] Unfortunately there was no prosecution initiated against perpetrators of such crimes.

---

[189] See Felix Reichlen, les Amerindiens et leur extermination deliberee, Pierre-Marcel Favre, 1987

[190] See David Svaldi, Sand Greek and the rhetoric of extermination, A case study in Indian-White relations, University Press of America, 1989

[191] See Antonio Cassese, International Criminal Law, Oxford University Press, 2003, p 67

Finally it was at the time of the aftermath of the WW1that the legal concept settled at both international military tribunals in Nuremberg and Tokyo respectively in their articles 6(C) and 5(C) define the concept of crime against humanity as:

> [N]amely, murder, extermination, enslavement, deportation and other inhuman acts committed against any civilian population, before to during the war, or persecutions on political, racial, religious grounds in execution of or in connection with any crime within the jurisdiction of the tribunal, whether or not in violation of the domestic law of the country where perpetrated.

Even though no one was tried for crimes against humanity by the Tokyo Tribunal, article 5(C) of the Charter of the Tokyo Tribunal adds an element of the criminal responsibility saying that:

> Leaders organisers, instigators and accomplices participating in the formulation or execution of a common plan or conspiracy to commit any or 'the foregoing crimes are responsible for all' acts performed by any person in execution of such plan.

5.2. Development through the International Law Commission

Already article 2(10) of the 1954 Draft Code of Offences against the Peace and Security of Mankind stipulated that the following acts are offences against peace and security of mankind:

> Inhuman acts such as murder, extermination, enslavement, deportation or persecutions, committed against any civilian population on social, political, racial, religious or cultural grounds by the authorities of a State or by private individuals acting at the instigation or with the toleration of such authorities.

It noteworthy to point out the observation made by the Yugoslavian representative in articulating an important element for the commission of such crimes in a systematic manner as follows:

> [L]es crimes contre l'humanite enumeres au paragraphe 10 doivent etre punis independamment du fait qu'ils aient ou non ete commis au cours de l'execution ou a l'occasion d'autres crimes definis a l'article 2 pourvu qu'ils soient perpetres "d'un maniere systematique."[192]

The concept of crimes against humanity was further revisited by the International Law Commission in 1991 as it considered non exhaustive the list of acts given in the 1954 Draft Code; it surprisingly removed certain crimes while adding up some others as hereunder discussed. Thus in its article 21, of the 1991 Draft Code of Crimes against the Peace and Security of Mankind providing for systematic or mass violation of human rights lists the following acts as constitutive of such crimes:

- Murder
- Torture
- Establishing or maintaining over persons a status of slavery, servitude or forced labor
- Persecution on social, political, racial, religious or cultural grounds in a systematic manner or on a mass scale; or
- Deportation or forcible transfer of population shall

The 1991 Draft Code commentary explained that the systematic element relates to the constant practice or to the planned methods used to carry out such crime. It further explained that the mass-scale could be established either by taking into consideration the number of victims affected or the geographical area where such crimes have been committed as one of these element could alternatively satisfy the requirement of the commission of the crimes against humanity.[193]

---

[192] See Yearbook of the International Law Commission, 1954, Vol. II, p 118
[193] See Yearbook of the International Law Commission, 1991, Vol. II Part II, p 103

Furthermore, the 1991 Draft Code should be commended for having added the crime of torture to the list; it however suffers a serious criticism for having removed the crime of extermination. The commentary to the article indicates that the Commission: "considered that extermination, where [extermination] was not a form of genocide, would constitute a form of mass murder and would thus be covered by the draft article."[194]

Such justification might be correct in the sense that a person who has committed the crime of extermination might still be charged under the crime of murder. However it fails to make a distinction between a person who has committed an act of murder as crime against humanity and a person who has committed –mass murder- or rather extermination as such.

Indeed in one case a single murder which occurs as part of systematic killing, would qualify as murder as crime against humanity without qualifying as extermination. On the other side, prosecuting extermination as murder dilutes such crime of its substantive element as it will be discussed later. Nevertheless this mistake was corrected by the 1996 Draft Code.

The 1996 Draft Code in its article 18 clarified its chapeau indicating it was providing for crimes against humanity as it added more offenses. Indeed it provides that:

> A crime against humanity means any of the following acts, when committed in a systematic manner or on a large scale and instigated or directed by a Government or by any organization or group:
> (a) Murder;
> (b) Extermination;
> (c) Torture;
> (d) Enslavement;
> (e) Persecution on political, racial, religious or ethnic grounds;
> (f) Institutionalized discrimination on racial, ethnic or religious grounds involving the violation of fundamental human rights and freedoms and resulting in seriously disadvantaging a part of the population;

194 See Yearbook of the International Law Commission, 1991, Vol. II Part II, p104

(g) Arbitrary deportation or forcible transfer of population;
(h) Arbitrary imprisonment;
(i) Forced disappearance of persons;
(j) Rape, enforced prostitution and other forms of sexual abuse;
(k) Other inhumane acts which severely damage physical or mental integrity, health or human dignity, such as mutilation and severe bodily harm

Certainly the Commission had taken into consideration the development made by various tribunals namely the Nuremberg Tribunal, the ICTY and the ICTR. Thus, amongst other things, the Commission added up more offences including discrimination, arbitrary imprisonment, forced disappearance but it also corrected the previously criticised removal of extermination by bringing it back on the list of offences under this crime. It further indicated that it was a settled rule of customary international law that crimes against humanity do not require a connection to international armed conflict.[195]

5.3 Development through the Nuremberg Tribunal

Some cases of the jurisprudence of the Nuremberg Tribunal could be considered as having contributed to the development of the concept of crimes against humanity. For instance the Justice Trial, clarified that the Tribunal had jurisdiction to try persons suspected for having committed crimes against humanity committed by Germans against fellow Germans or stateless persons. [196]

Whereas the Flick Trial declined to consider compulsory taking of individual property as part of crime against humanity reasoning that the wording "other persecutions" must be deemed to include only crimes affecting the life and liberty of the oppressed peoples.[197]

---

[195] See Report of the International Law Commission on the work of its forty-eighth session, p 48
[196] See Law report of trials of war criminals selected and prepared by the United Nations War Crimes Commission, Vol. VI, p 40
[197] Idem, Vol. IX, p 28

However it is interesting to note that in the same Flick trial, the Tribunal declined to make a general declaration that acts committed before 1939 were crimes against humanity within the meaning of the Charter. Indeed the International Military Tribunal found that it could hardly have decided that no crime against humanity could possibly have been committed before the war, because Article 6(c) of the Charter includes the words" before or during the war" which governs that provision.[198]

Generally in international criminal there is no nexus required between the crime of crimes against humanity and the existence of an armed conflict. The Nuremberg Tribunal declined to make any general statement in that respect as matter of jurisdictional limitation of its particular Charter. As it was created purposely to try crimes which were committed in circumstances related to a particular armed conflict thus having it jurisdiction limited exclusively to crimes related to a given situation limited within a given time framework.

Nevertheless the Control Council Law No. 10 clarified in its Art. (1) c according to which ... as it removed the nexus requirement to the war.

5.4 Nexus Requirement to an Armed Conflict

As indicated earlier, the provision of the Nuremberg and Tokyo Charters required crimes against humanity to be connected to the aggressive war, however the Control Council Law No. 10 Art II 1 C[199] left out such requirement. Furthermore, Art 5 of the ICTY Statute requires that such crimes must occur in connection to the armed conflict, though Art 3 of the ICTR Statute does not require a link to armed conflict.

---

[198] Idem, p 48

[199] It provides that Crimes against Humanity. Atrocities and offenses, including but not limited to murder, extermination, enslavement, deportation, imprisonment, torture, rape, or other inhumane acts committed against any civilian population, or persecutions on political, racial or religious grounds whether or not in violation of the domestic laws of the country where perpetrated

As clarified in the Akayesu Case,[200] the requirement that limits the jurisdiction of Tribunal to crime against humanity committed within given circumstances namely at the time of war, however such limitation is by no means to be replicated in the definition of the crime against humanity as understood in international law.

Thus, in general, international law does not require the commission of crimes against humanity to be connected to an armed conflict. Indeed massive human rights violations committed against a given population could amount to crimes against humanity even when such crimes are committed in time of peace. Furthermore, even when a crime against humanity is committed in the context of an armed conflict, it is immaterial whether the crime has a nexus to the armed conflict.[201]

5.5 Position of the Current Ad hoc Tribunals

In its article 3 the Statute of the ICTR which provides for Crimes against Humanity stipulates that:

> The International Tribunal for Rwanda shall have the power to prosecute persons responsible for the following crimes when committed as part of a widespread or systematic attack against any civilian population on national, political, ethnic, racial or religious grounds:
> (a) Murder;
> (b) Extermination;
> (c) Enslavement;
> (d) Deportation;
> (e) Imprisonment;
> (f) Torture;
> (g) Rape;

[200] See Jean-Paul Akayesu Appeals Judgement, para 464
[201] Roger O' Keefe, International Criminal Law, Oxford University Press, 2015, p 143

(h) Persecutions on political, racial and religious grounds;
(i) Other inhumane acts.[202]

The particularity of the crime against humanity is that its structure requires a combination of three factors. The material which consists of the commission of one or more acts prohibited by the law as such, the mental element requiring intent to commit such a particular crime and the contextual element[203] which is satisfied when such act is committed in the course of a wide spread or systematic attack against a given civilian population as discussed below and the required mens rea.

5.5.1 Elements of the Crime

The actus reus of crime against humanity requires the commission of one or more of the following acts: murder, extermination, enslavement,

[202] A similar provision is found in article 5 of the ICTY Statute mutatis mutandis. Whereas the Rome Statute rather provides that:
1. For the purpose of this Statute, 'crime against humanity' means any of the following acts when committed as part of a widespread or systematic attack directed against any civilian population, with knowledge of the attack:
(a) Murder;
(b) Extermination;
(c) Enslavement;
(d) Deportation or forcible transfer of population;
(e) Imprisonment or other severe deprivation of physical liberty in violation of fundamental rules of international law;
(f) Torture;
(g) Rape, sexual slavery, enforced prostitution, forced pregnancy, enforced sterilization, or any other form of sexual violence of comparable gravity;
(h) Persecution against any identifiable group or collectivity on political, racial, national, ethnic, cultural, religious, gender as defined in paragraph 3, or other grounds that are universally recognized as impermissible under international law, in connection with any act referred to in this paragraph or any crime within the jurisdiction of the Court;
(i) Enforced disappearance of persons;
(j) The crime of apartheid;
(k) Other inhumane acts of a similar character intentionally causing great suffering, or serious injury to body or to mental or physical health.

[203] Gerhard Werle and Florian Jessberger, Principles of International Criminal Law, 3rd ed. Oxford University Press, 2014, p 333

deportation, imprisonment, torture, rape, persecutions and other inhumane acts. Though the mens rea for each crime forming part of crimes against humanity is distinctive, in general terms, the Kunarac case determined that:

> [T]he accused must have had the intent to commit the underlying offence or offences with which he is charged, and that he must have known "that there is an attack on the civilian population and that his acts comprise part of that attack, or at least [that he took] the risk that his acts were part of the attack.[204]

Concerning the contextual element, in the Tihomir case the Appeals Chamber said that the concept of widespread attacks would refer to the large-scale, the number of victims of the attack, the concept of systematic attacks would refer to the organized nature of the acts of violence and the improbability of their random occurrence. The Chamber explained that "the non-accidental repetition of similar criminal conduct on a regular basis"[205] constitutes the patterns which prove its systematic nature.

It should be indicated that the contextual elements is met when any of the two elements are met either alternatively or jointly. Indeed article 3 of the ICTR Statute requires that such crimes be committed as part of a widespread or systematic attack. Thus either of the two would be considered satisfactory provided sporadic occurrence of certain crimes is not taken for crimes against humanity.

Though the list of prohibited acts for crimes against humanity comprises of nine crimes, considering the context of the case study, this research will focus only on murder and extermination as crimes against humanity as other crimes fall outside the scope of the current case.

[204] See ICTY, Kunarac et al. Trial Judgement, para 102
[205] See ICTY,Blaskic Tihomir Apeals Judgement, para 101

5.5.2 Murder

5.5.2.1 Actus Reus

In the Krajisnik case, though the Trial Chamber held that murder as a crime against humanity requires proof that the accused caused the victim's death.[206] For the purposes of such crime, the surrounding circumstance of the death of victim requires a close analysis. Thus in its first case of murder as a crime against humanity, the Trial Chamber in Akayesu defined murder as an unlawful, intentional killing of a human being, explaining that the required material element is that the victim is dead, and that the death resulted from an unlawful act or omission of the accused.[207]

However in the Kayishema case, the Trial Chamber noted that Article 3(a) of the English version of the Statute uses the term murder, whilst the French version of the Statute uses the term assassinat. The Defence argued that murder was meant to be the equivalent of assassinat,while the Prosecution argued that premeditation was not a necessary element and suggested that the threshold of the murder in this case be lowered to "unlawful killing of a human being as the result of the perpetrator engaging in conduct which was in reckless disregard for human life" be considered enough.[208]

It isn't clear whether the submission of the Prosecution to include recklessness would mean homicide involontaire, which per se is a result of negligence, recklessness, lack of precaution would also be considered a crime against humanity. If the Prosecution would have meant murder to be understood as meurtre, the concept of recklessness would not apply as meurtre is rather considered the fact of killing with the intention or usually referred as homicide intentionelle. The difference with assassinat which is also homicide volontaire but requires an element of premeditation. Among other things, premeditation can be proven for instance by the fact that the accused did set a trap, guet-apens, the fact for the accused to have taken time to think about the crime, to plan its careful execution…

---

[206] See ICTY, Krajisnik Momcilo Trial Judgement, para 1130
[207] See ICTR, Jean-Paul Akayesu Trial Judgement, para 589
[208] See ICTR, Clement Kayishema Trial Judgement, para 137

Nevertheless, the Trial Chamber decided in favour of the Defence as it found that by using assassinat in French, the drafters may have intended that only the higher standards of mens rea for murder would suffice.[209] The Trial Chamber concluded that the actus reus of the crime of murder is rather met if the accused, engaging in conduct which is unlawful, causes the death of another by a premeditated act or omission.[210]

However the reasoning of the Trial Chamber might hardly be understood as it stated that: "Although it may be argued that, under customary international law, it is murder rather than assassinat that constitutes the crime against humanity." This position would be hardly considered as customary international law though the Trial Chamber cited the Akayesu case, without any proof that this was customary law. But perhaps more worrisome would be the ambiguous statement that "the ICTR and ICTY Statutes did not reflect customary international law at the time of drafting."[211]

The reasoning of the Trial Chamber was that the inclusion of the nexus to the armed conflict in the ICTY Statute and the inclusion of the requirement that the crimes be committed with discriminatory intent in the ICTR Statute constituted evidence that these Tribunals Statutes did not reflect customary law.

These statements could raise a number of questions including whether the Akayesu case itself reflected customary law, and whether the Trial Chamber was therefore entitled to disregard customary law for reasons given in the judgment. The opposite might rather sound more accurate.

Thankfully the ICTR in the majority of its decisions abandoned the discussion on meurtre/assassinat as it settled for the definition of murder as "the intentional killing of a person without any lawful justification or excuse or the intentional infliction of grievous bodily harm leading to death with knowledge that such harm will likely cause the victim's death."[212]

---

[209] Idem, para 138
[210] Idem, para 140
[211] Idem, para 138
[212] See Bagosora et al., TC 2169, Karera TC, para. 558

5.5.2.2 Mens Rea

As discussed earlier the difference between the meurtrevolontaire and meurtre involontaire is the intention of the accused. Assassinat would therefore require that the accused intends to kill. In the Akayesu case the Trial Chamber held that at the time of the killing the accused must have the intention to kill or inflict grievous bodily harm on the deceased having known that such bodily harm is likely to cause the victim's death.[213]

However the specific aspect of the mens rea for murder as a crime against humanity is that such mens rea is double folded in the sense that it requires an accumulation of two elements, that is, the accused must have the intention to kill the victim but must also have the knowledge that his criminal conduct is part of a widespread or systematic plan to kill a certain group of people without which element the contextual element cannot be met.

It is in this respect that an accused person could be charged of murder as a crime against humanity even in the case that they have killed a single person provided the contextual element is met. For instance in the Ntakirutimana case the Trial Chamber found the accused guilty of murder of Charles Ukobizaba, a single victim but who was killed as part of a widespread and systematic attack.[214]

5.5.3 Extermination

5.5.3.1 The Concept

As pointed out by the International Law Commission, during its 48th session of 1996, extermination is a crime which by its nature is directed against a group of individuals.[215] The material element of extermination is

[213] Akayesu TC 589
[214] Ntakirutimana TC 810
[215] See Report of the International Law Commission on the work of its forty-eighth session, 1996, p 48

the mass killing of a substantial number of civilians.[216] This crime requires an element of human mass destruction. Extermination can be committed in a direct way that is by killing the victims or by causing serious bodily harm in the reasonable knowledge that it was likely to result in death as it can happen in an indirect fashion.

Though the Statutes of the ad hoc Tribunals do not specifically provide for indirect commission of the crime of extermination as the Rome Statute does in its article 7(2)(b), such concept has been however accepted by the jurisprudence of these Tribunals. Thus in the Brdanin case the Trial Chamber found that a conduct which creates conditions provoking the victim's death and ultimately mass killings, such as the deprivation of food and medicine, or subjecting a certain population to a certain condition of life calculated to cause the destruction of part of the population would amount to the crime of extermination.[217]

5.5.3.2 Structure of the Crime

As indicated earlier the crime of extermination is constituted by mass killing of civilian population. Its actus reus is the act of killing on a large scale. This is distinguished from murder by the fact that it is committed massively. Its mens rea is constituted by the intention of the accused "to kill on a large scale or to systematically subject a large number of people to conditions of living that would lead to their deaths."[218] Its contextual element requires that the accused commits such crime as part of a widespread or systematic attack directed against a civilian population as discussed bellow.

---

[216] See ICTR, Laurent Semanza Trial Judgement, para 463

[217] See ICTY, Radoslav Brdanin Trial Judgement, para 389; The same was held in the Krstic Trila Judgement, para 503 in which the Trial Chamber found that: "[I]n addition to the general requirements for a crime against humanity, there must be evidence that a particular population was targeted and that its members were killed or otherwise subjected to conditions of life calculated to bring about the destruction of a numerically significant part of the population."

[218] Lukic AC 536 see also Ntakirutimana Appeal Judgement, para. 522, Here the ICTY dealt with the question of the definition of the crime of extermination in the case of Stakic Milimir. It then adopted of the ICTR Appeal Chambers according to which the accused must have accused participated in a widespread or systematic killing or in subjecting a widespread number of people or systematically subjecting a number of people to conditions of living that would inevitably lead to death (actus reus), and that the accused intended by his acts or omissions this result (mens rea).

5.5.3.3 Actus Reus

It is well settled in international criminal law that sporadic or isolated cases of killings cannot constitute crime against humanity. Though, international jurisprudence recognizes that the concept of large scale does not require a strict numerical approach with a minimum and/or maximum number of victims.[219]

Indeed in the Ndahimana case, the Appeals Chamber after having recalled that the crime against humanity has been found in relation to the killing of thousands of persons, as it has been found in relation to fewer killings, such as the killings of approximately 60 individuals and less.[220] The same Chamber confirmed that: "a particularly large number of victims can be considered an aggravating circumstance in relation to the sentence for this crime if the extent of the killings exceeds that required for extermination."[221]

The Trial Chamber had found that the number of victims of the attack on Nyange church, for which Ndahimana is individually responsible, was an aggravating factor[222] which could not be considered impermissible double-counting as suggested by the defence.

It should be noted that though the Appeal Chamber never stated which number should be considered as exceeding the requirement for extermination the Chamber confirmed the Trial Chamber sentence had considered 2000 victims as an aggravating circumstance.

Thus, as said in Nyiramasuhuko case, the assessment of large scale killing must be done on a case-by-case basis, however due consideration should be given to various circumstances surrounding the killings including time of the killings, place of the killings, criteria of selection of the victims and the manner in which victims were killed, whether they were target as group or whether they have been killed individually.[223]

---

[219] See ICTY, Lukic Appeals Judgement, para 537

[220] See ICTR, Gregoire Ndahimana Appeals Judgement, para 231

[221] Idem

[222] See ICTR, Gregoire Ndahimana Trial Judgement, para 860

[223] See ICTR, Pauline Nyiramasuhuko Appeals Judgement, para 2123; In Stakić, the Trial Chamber found that the killing of less than 80 individuals "independently would reach the requisite level of massiveness for the purposes of an evaluation under Article 5(b) of the Statute". In Krajišnik, while

Indeed, for an act of killing to be considered as extermination, it has to be done on a massive scale or be done as part of massive killing. Much that all crimes against humanity require a contextual element for them to qualify as such, the crime of extermination is so typical in the sense that the requirement of the collective nature of the crime is at play without which element the crime cannot be committed.

As the difference with the crime of murder which would remain a crime even in the context of a single isolated killing though without qualifying as a crime against humanity, extermination happens only in a massive context as random and/or selected killings are excluded from this crime. Here one could conclude that the contextual element becomes part of the material elements.

5.5.3.4 Mens Rea

In the Stanisic and Zupljanin case, the Appeals Chamber held that:

> [I]t has consistently held that the elements of the crime of extermination are the same as those required for murder as a crime against humanity, with the difference that extermination is killing on a large scale. As such, the Appeals Chamber considers that the mens rea for extermination to
>
> > "(i) kill on a large scale" can be met by establishing the mens rea for murder as a crime against humanity – i.e. the intent to kill the victim; or
> > (ii) wilfully cause serious bodily harm which the perpetrator should reasonably have known might lead to death
> > –plus the additional intention to do so on a large scale.[224]

---

the conviction for extermination as a crime against humanity was based on the killing of at least 1,916 individuals, the Trial Chamber found that the killing of approximately 66 individuals during the Pionirska Street Incident satisfied the element of massiveness. See also ICTY, Lukic Appeals Judgement, para 537

[224] See ICTY, Mico Stanisic and Stojan Zupljanin Appeals Judgement, para 1036; The same was held in Krstic as the Trial Chamber held that offences of murder and extermination have a similar elements, that is they both intend the death of the victims as they have the same mens rea, which consists of the intention to kill or the intention to cause serious bodily injury to the victim which the perpetrator must have reasonably foreseen was likely to result in death. See ICTY, Krstic Trial Judgement, para 495

The same reasoning is found in the Stakic case as the Appeal Chamber highlighted the requirement of the intention to kill on a large scale or to systematically subject a large number of people to conditions of living that would lead to their deaths,[225] which according to the Appeal Chamber must be a clear reflection of the actus reus.[226]

5.5.3.5 The Contextual Element

As explained by professor Cassese, Crimes against humanity are not isolated or sporadic acts.[227] They must be committed on a widespread scale, that is the requirement that such crimes are committed in a systematic fashion. Though no legal prescription provies for the ties that has to exist between the criminal and the government, such crimes occur frequently when they are committed by state officials, sponsored or tolerated by a given government which exercises its authority either de jure or defacto.

Thus as it was concluded by the international law commission the possibility for private individuals with de facto power or organized in criminal gangs might also commit systematic crimes is not ruled out.[228]

Furthermore, widespread can be derived from the extension over a broad geographic area as it can also derive from the number of victims.[229] Thus spontaneous and isolated crimes are not to be considered systematic. However this does not mean that an individual who perpetrates a single offense mentioned on the list of the prohibited acts or an individual who commit such acts against a few civilians cannot be prosecuted for the same. It rather suffices that such punctual acts are committed as part of the widespread for the contextual element to be satisfied.

---

[225] See ICTY, Milomir Stakic Appeals Judgement, para 260
[226] Idem, para 554
[227] See Antonio Cassese, International Criminal Law, Oxford University Press, 2003, p 64
[228] See Yearbook of the International Law Commission, Vol. II, Part II, 1991, p 104
[229] See for instance the 1996 Draft Code

CONCLUDING REMARKS: THE RUTAGANIRA CASE

The facts which gave rise to the case are that Tutsi had taken refuge in churches including the Mubuga Church. However these displaced civilians were killed at the place where they had sought shelter.[230] Since the facts were not disputed, the Defence and the Prosecution agreed on the crime of extermination.

However in the Kayishema and Ruzindana cases from which the Rutaganira case was disjointed the Trial Chamber found that these crimes were committed against people belonging to the Tutsi ethnic group with the intent to destroy this group in whole or in part. The Trial Chamber retained that qualification of genocide.[231]

It could be recalled that the initial indictment had charged Mr. Rutaganira of the crime of genocide, crimes against humanity amongst others.[232] The amendment to the charges which followed the guilty plea agreement might have benefited the Accused because of the discount of such crimes, including the crime of genocide as already discussed.

[230] See ICTR, Vincent Rutaganira Trial Judgement, para 32
[231] See ICTR, Kayishema and Ruzindana Trial Judgement, paras 277 - 279
[232] See ICTR, The prosecutor against Clement Kayishema et al. First Amended Indictment p. 9

SELECTED READINGS

Antonio Cassese, International Criminal Law, Oxford University Press, 2003

Chaim Clorfene and Yaakov Rogalsky, The Path of the Righteous Gentile: A Practical Guide to the Seven Laws of Noah, CreateSpace Independent Publishing Platform, 2016

David Svaldi, Sand Greek and the rhetoric of extermination, A case study in Indian-White relations, University Press of America, 1989

Elies Van Sliedregt, Individual criminal responsibility in international law, Oxford University Press, 2012

Felix Reichlen, Les Amerindiens et leur extermination deliberee, Pierre-Marcel Favre, 1987

Gerhard Werle and Florian Jessberger, Principles of International Criminal Law, 3rd ed. Oxford University Press, 2014

Gideon Boas, 'Omission Liability in International Criminal Law - A Case for Reform', in Shane Darcy and Joseph Powderly, in Judicial Creativity at the International Criminal Tribunals, Oxford University Press, 2011

Hector Olasolo and Enrique Carnero Rojo, Forms of accessorial Liability under Art 25(3) and (c), in Carsten Stahn, The law and practice of the international criminal court, Oxford University Press, 2015

ICTR, OTP, Complementarity in action: Lessons learned from the ICTR Prosecutor's referral of international criminal cases to national jurisdictions for trial, 2015

James G. Stewart, The end of "Modes of Liability" for international Crimes" in Leiden Journal of international Law, 2012
Jessie Ingle, Aiding and abetting by omission before the International Criminal tribunals, in Journal of International Criminal Justice, 2016

Kai Ambos, Modes of criminal responsibility, in Max Planck Encyclopaedia of International Law, 2013

Olivera Simic´, "I Would Do the Same Again": In Conversation With Biljana Plavsic, in International Criminal Justice Review, Georgia State University, 2018

Regina E. Rauxloh, Plea bargaining in international criminal justice: Can the International Criminal Court afford to avoid trials? In The Journal of Criminal Justice Research, 2011

Roger O' Keefe, International Criminal Law, Oxford University Press, 2015

FURTHER READINGS

Alexandra Orlova and James Moore, "Umbrellas" or "Building Blocks"?: Defining International Terrorism and Transnational Organized Crime in International Law in Houston Journal of International Law, 2005

Andre Vartan Armenian, "Selectivity in International Criminal Law: An Assessment of the 'Progress Narrative'", in International Criminal Law Review, 2016

Anthony Anghie and B. S. Chimni, Third World Approaches to International Law and Individual Responsibility in Internal Armed Conflict, in Chinese Journal of International Law, 2003

Carsten Stahn and Göran Sluiter (eds.), The Emerging Practice of the International Criminal Court, Martinus Nirjhof Publishers, 2009

Cesare Romano, and others (eds.), Internationalized Criminal Courts - Sierra Leone, East Timor, Kosovo, and Cambodia, Oxford University Press, 2004

Cherif Bassiouni (ed.), International Criminal Law, Transnational Pub Inc, 1986

Fred C. Zacharias, Structuring the Ethics of Prosecutorial Trial Practice: Can Prosecutors Do Justice?, in Vanderbilt Law Review, 1991

Immi Tallgren, The Sense and Sensibility of International Criminal Law, in European Journal of International Law, 2002

Jann K. Kleffner, Complementarity in the Rome Statute and National Criminal Jurisdictions, Oxford University Press, 2008

Jean Galbraith, The Pace of International Justice, in Michigan Journal of International Law, 2009

Kai Ambos and Ignaz Stegmiller, Prosecuting international crimes at the International Criminal Court: is there a coherent and comprehensive prosecution strategy? Springer, 2013

Kai Ambos, Treatise on International Criminal Law: Vol. III: International Criminal Procedure, Oxford University Press, 2016

Kenneth Gallant, The principle of legality in international and comparative law, Cambridge University Press, 2009

Mark Drumbl, Atrocity, Punishment and International Law, Cambridge University Press, 2007

Mark Freeman, Necessary Evils: Amnesties and the Search for Justice, Cambridge University Press, 2009

Markus Benzing, International Criminal Court: International Criminal Justice between State Sovereignty and the Fight against Impunity in Max Planck Yearbook of United Nations Law, 2003

Martti Koskenniemi, Between Impunity and Show Trials, in Max Planck Yearbook of United Nations Law, 2006

Mirjan Damaška, What is the Point of International Criminal Justice, in Chicago-Kent Law Review, 2008

Reinhold Gallmetzer, Prosecuting Persons Doing Business with Armed Groups in Conflict Areas, in Journal of International Criminal Justice, 2010
Robert Cryer and others, An Introduction to International Criminal Law and Procedure, Cambridge University Press, 2010

Roger Clark, Offences of International Concern: Multilateral Treaty Practice in the Forty Years since Nuremberg in Nordic Journal of International Law, 1988

Ward N.Ferdinandusse, Direct Application of International Criminal Law in National Courts, Cambridge University Press, 2006

International Criminal Tribunal for Rwanda
Tribunal pénal international pour le Rwanda

TRIAL CHAMBER III

Case No. ICTR-95-1C-T

ENGLISH
Original: FRENCH

Before: Judge Andrésia Vaz, presiding
Judge Flavia Lattanzi
Judge Florence Rita Arrey

Registrar: Adama Dieng

Date delivered: 14 March 2005

THE PROSECUTOR

v.

VINCENT RUTAGANIRA

JUDGEMENT AND SENTENCE

Office of the Prosecutor:
Charles Adeogun-Phillips
Wallace Kapaya
Renifa Madenga
Maymuchka Lauriston
Florida Kabasinga

Counsel for the Defence:
François Roux
Maroufa Diabira
Soraya Brikci-Laucci

CIII05-0020 (E)
Translation certified by LSS, ICTR

TABLE OF CONTENTS

CHAPTER I: INTRODUCTION 113

A. The Tribunal and its jurisdiction 113

B. The Accused 113

C. Proceedings 114

CHAPTER II: THE GUILTY PLEA 117

A. The applicable law 117

B. The Chamber's consideration of the validity of the guilty plea by the Accused 119

CHAPTER III: THE EVENTS 121

CHAPTER IV: CRIMINAL RESPONSIBILITY OF THE ACCUSED ON THE COUNT OF EXTERMINATION AS A CRIME AGAINST HUMANITY (COUNT 16 OF THE INDICTMENT)...127

A. Extermination as a crime against humanity (Article 3(b) of the Statute of the Tribunal) 128
   1. The massacres at Mubuga church between 14 and 17 April 1994 128
   2. Widespread and systematic attack 129
   3. The civilian population targeted on ethnic grounds 130

B. Participation of the Accused Vincent Rutaganira in the crime of extermination (crime against humanity) through complicity by omission 130
   1. Actus reus 132
   2. Mens rea 138

C. Findings 140

CHAPTER V: INDIVIDUAL CRIMINAL RESPONSIBILITY OF THE ACCUSED ON COUNTS 1, 14, 15, 17, 18 AND 19 141

A. Submissions of the Parties 141

B. Findings 142

CHAPTER VI: VERDICT 143

CHAPTER VII: DETERMINATION OF PENALTIES 145

A. Sentencing principles 145

B. Factors to be taken into account 148
1. Gravity of the crime 148
2. Individual circumstance 149
2.1 Family circumstance 149
2.2 Personality and general conduct of the Accused 150
2.3 Lack of a criminal record and good conduct while in detention 151
2.4 Old age and sickness 152
2.5 No active participation in the killings 153
3. Aggravating Circumtances 153
4. Mitigating Circumstances 155
4.1 Voluntary surrender 155
4.2 Guilty plea 155
4.3 Assistance provided to certain victims 157
4.4 Remorse 157
4.5 Duress 158
5. General practice regarding prison sentences in Rwanda 159

C. Sentencing 160
1. Findings 161
2. Credit for time served 161

CHAPTER VIII: DISPOSITION 163

CHAPTER I: INTRODUCTION

A. The Tribunal and its jurisdiction

1. This Judgement is delivered by Trial Chamber III (the "Chamber") of the International Criminal Tribunal for Rwanda (the "Tribunal") in the case of The Prosecutor v. Vincent Rutaganira.

2. The Tribunal was established by United Nations Security Council Resolution 955 of 8 November 1994 with a mandate for "prosecuting persons responsible for genocide and other serious violations of International Humanitarian Law committed in the territory of Rwanda and Rwandan citizens responsible for genocide and other such violations committed in the territory of neighbouring States, between 1 January 1994 and 31 December 1994".[1]

3. The jurisdiction ratione materiae of the Tribunal covers genocide, crimes against humanity, serious violations of Article 3 Common to the four Geneva Conventions and of Additional Protocol II thereto, with its personal jurisdiction being limited to natural persons.

B. The Accused

4. The Accused Vincent Rutaganira was born in 1944 in Mubuga, Gishyita commune, Kibuye préfecture, Rwanda. He is married and a father to 10 children. He underwent a twoyear technical training course in motor mechanics and another training course in traditional medicine graduating as a herbalist.[2]

[1] S/RES/955, 8 November 1994. The Tribunal is governed by the Statute as amended by Security Council Resolutions 1165, 1329, 1411, 1431, 1503 and 1512.
[2] T.8 December 2004, p. 6.

5. Vincent Rutaganira was elected conseiller communal of Mubuga secteur in 1985 and served up to the end of July 1994.[3] Therefore the Accused was holding office at the time of the events which gave rise to the crimes charged.

C. Proceedings

6. On 22 November 1995, the Prosecutor filed an initial Indictment which was confirmed by Judge Navanethem Pillay on 28 November 1995.

7. On 12 December 1995, an arrest warrant and a transfer request were transmitted to the Justice Minister of Zaire where Vincent Rutaganira was allegedly residing.

8. On 6 May 1996, the Trial Chamber granted the Prosecution's request to amend its Indictment.[4]

9. The Prosecutor charged Vincent Rutaganira with eight counts: Conspiracy to commit genocide (Count 1), Genocide (Count 14), Murder as crime against humanity (Count 15), Extermination as crime against humanity (Count 16), other inhumane acts as crimes against humanity (Count 17) Serious Violations of Article 3 Common to the Geneva Conventions (Count 18) and Serious Violations of Additional Protocol II thereto (Count 19).

10. On 18 February 2002, an arrest warrant issued against Vincent Rutaganira was sent to all Member States of the United Nations. On 4 March 2002, the Accused surrendered voluntarily to the Tribunal and was transferred on the same day to the Detention Facility of the Tribunal.

11. The initial appearance on 7 March 2002 was adjourned at the request of the Prosecution and the Defence.[5]

---

[3] T.17 January 2005, p. 12.

[4] The Prosecutor v. Clément Kayishema, Ignace Bagilishema, Charles Sikubwabo, Aloys N'Dimbati, Vincent Rutaganira, Mika Muhimana, Ryandikayo and Obed Ruzindana, Order to Amend the Indictment of 6 May 1996.

[5] T.7 March 2002, pp. 8-11; p. 13.

12. At his initial appearance on 26 March 2002, the Accused pleaded not guilty to all the counts.[6]

13. At a status conference held on 17 September 2004, the Prosecution asserted that it had sent a letter to the Defence as part of negotiations on the proceedings against Vincent Rutaganira. The Prosecution asserted that "the result of those ongoing negotiations may or could save a substantial amount of time".[7]

14. At a status conference held on 8 December 2004, the Prosecution and Vincent Rutaganira informed the Chamber that they had reached a plea agreement on 7 December 2004.[8]

15. At a new appearance hearing held on 8 December 2004, Vincent Rutaganira indeed pleaded guilty to the charge of complicity by omission in the crime of extermination (crime against humanity) under Article 3(b) of the Statute of the Tribunal, as charged in Count 16 of the Indictment. However, he pleaded not guilty to the remaining counts.[9]

16. The Prosecutor requested the Chamber to admit the guilty plea, to find the Accused guilty under Count 16, to dismiss Counts 1, 14, 15, 17, 18 and 19 for lack of evidence and to acquit him on the said counts.[10]

17. The Chamber found the guilty plea of Vincent Rutaganira sincere and valid and took note of the Prosecutor's request.[11]

18. At the request of the Defence, the Chamber subsequently agreed to hear three character witnesses.

---

[6] T.26 March 2002, p. 15 (French).
[7] T.17 September 2004, p. 3.
[8] T. 2004, p. 2. On the same day, the two parties filed three documents with the Registry: "Accord de reconnaissance de culpabilité conclu entre M. Vincent Rutaganira et le Bureau du Procureur", "Requête conjointe visant à l'examen d'un Accord entre Vincent Rutaganira et le Bureau du Procureur aux fins d'un plaidoyer de culpabilité" and a " Mémoire conjoint entre Vincent Rutaganira et le Bureau du Procureur préalable au prononcé de la sentence" ("Mémoire conjoint").
[9] T.8 December 2004, pp. 7-9.
[10] Ibid., p. 3.
[11] Ibid., pp. 12-13.

19. At a 17 January 2005 hearing, the Prosecutor, on the one hand, sought severance of Vincent Rutaganira's trial from that of the other accused persons named in the Indictment of 6 May 1996 and, on the other hand, reiterated his request for dismissal of and acquittal on all counts except for Count 16.[12]

20. The Defence sought rectification to the plea agreement which would result in only the words "omissions" being retained with the term "acts" being struck. It also prayed the Chamber to keep said Agreement confidential, except for its Chapters V and VI.

21. The Chamber ordered that Vincent Rutaganira's trial be severed from that of the other accused persons named in the Indictment of 6 May 1996 and directed the Registrar to assign a new number to the case. Furthermore, after granting the Defence's request for rectification, the Chamber ordered disclosure in closed session of the guilty plea agreement, except for Chapters V and VI, on security grounds and pursuant to Rule 62bis of the Rules. Subsequently, the Defence read out Chapters V and VI of said Agreement in open court.[13]

22. At the request of the Defence, the Chamber also requested the medical officer of the Detention Facility to produce under seal a medical report on the Accused.[14]

23. The Chamber further admitted into the record written statements by other nonappearing witnesses (TRV-6, TRV-9 and TRV-10).[15]

24. In closing arguments, the Prosecutor pleaded both the aggravating and mitigating circumstances to be considered by the Chamber in determining the sentence to be imposed on the Accused.[16]

25. On the other hand, the Defence pleaded circumstances in mitigation.[17] In this regard, it called its three character witnesses.[18]

---

[12] T.17 January 2005, p. 2
[13] Ibid., p. 24.
[14] The medical report on Vincent Rutaganira's health was prepared and submitted to the Chamber on 20 January 2005.
[15] T.17 January 2005, p. 17.
[16] Ibid., pp. 6-10.
[17] Ibid., pp. 35-42.
[18] Ibid., pp. 18-31.

CHAPTER II:

THE GUILTY PLEA

A. The applicable law

26. The Statute does not directly address guilty pleas. The relevant provisions, namely Rule 62(B) and Rule 62bis of the Rules of Procedure and Evidence provide as follows:

Rule 62: Initial Appearance of Accused and Plea

(A) Upon his transfer to the Tribunal, the accused shall be brought before a Trial Chamber or a Judge thereof without delay, and shall be formally charged. The Trial Chamber or the Judge shall:

(i) Satisfy itself or himself that the right of the accused to counsel is respected;
(ii) Read or have the indictment read to the accused in a language he speaks and understands, and satisfy itself or himself that the accused understands the indictment;
(iii) Call upon the accused to enter a plea of guilty or not guilty on each count; should the accused fail to do so, enter a plea of not guilty on his behalf;
(iv) In case of a plea of not guilty, instruct the Registrar to set a date for trial;
(v) In case of a plea of guilty:

(a) if before a Judge, refer the plea to the Trial Chamber so that it may act in accordance with Rule 62 (B); or
(b) if before a Trial Chamber, act in accordance with Rule 62 (B).

(B) If an accused pleads guilty in accordance with Rule 62 (A)(v), or requests to change his plea to guilty, the Trial Chamber shall satisfy itself that the guilty plea:

(i) is made freely and voluntarily;
(ii) is an informed plea;
(iii) is unequivocal; and
(iv) is based on sufficient facts for the crime and accused's participation in it, either on the basis of objective indicia or of lack of any material disagreement between the parties about the facts of the case.

Thereafter the Trial Chamber may enter a finding of guilt and instruct the Registrar to set a date for the sentencing hearing.

Rule 62bis: Plea Agreement Procedure

(A) The Prosecutor and the Defence may agree that, upon the accused entering a plea of guilty to the indictment or to one or more counts of the indictment, the Prosecutor shall do one or more of the following before the Trial Chamber:

(i) apply to amend the indictment accordingly;
(ii) submit that a specific sentence or sentencing range is appropriate;
(iii) not oppose a request by the accused for a particular sentence or sentencing range.

(B) The Trial Chamber shall not be bound by any agreement specified in paragraph (A).

(C) If a plea agreement has been reached by the parties, the Trial Chamber shall require the disclosure of the agreement in open session or, on a showing of good cause, in closed session, at the time the accused pleads guilty in accordance with Rule 62 (A) (v), or requests to change his or her plea to guilty.

B. The Chamber's consideration of the validity of the guilty plea by the Accused

27. Following a reading of the charges by the Registrar at a new appearance hearing on 8 December 2005, Vincent Rutaganira pleaded guilty to the crime against humanity (extermination) referred to in Count 16 of the Indictment, thereby confining his plea to complicity by omission.[19]

28. Pursuant to Rule 62(B)(i) to (iii) of the Rules, the Chamber proceeded to satisfy itself of the validity of the said guilty plea. In so doing, it asked the Accused if his plea was voluntary, if he had made it freely, knowingly and without coercion, threat or promise; if the Accused had understood well the nature of the charges and the consequences of his plea; if he was aware that the guilty plea was incompatible with any grounds of defence; if he had indeed signed the Agreement containing his plea. The Accused having responded in the affirmative to all these questions, the Chamber found the guilty plea of Vincent Rutaganira to have been done freely and voluntarily, to have been an informed, unequivocal and sincere plea.

29. In the light of Chapter V of the guilty plea agreement, and in the absence of any disagreement between the Prosecutor and the Accused as to the facts of the case, the Chamber, acting pursuant to Rule 62bis(B)(iv), also found that the guilty plea of the Accused Vincent Rutaganira relied on sufficient facts to establish both the crime against humanity (extermination), referred to in Count 16 of the Indictment and the participation of the Accused for having abetted such a crime by omission.

30. In light of the foregoing findings, the Chamber found the guilty plea of Vincent Rutaganira valid.[20]

---

[19] T.December 2004, pp. 7-98.
[20] T.8 December 2004, pp. 12-13.

CIII05-0020 (E)
Translation certified by LSS, ICTR

CHAPTER III:

THE EVENTS

31. From 1985 to 1994, the Accused was conseiller communal of Mubuga secteur in Gishyita commune, Kibuye préfecture[21] and was as such responsible for the economic, social and cultural development of his secteur.[22] As a prominent member of the community and by virtue of his office, Vincent Rutaganira served as a link between the inhabitants and the local political structures in this secteur. [23]

32. The Accused knew, on the one hand, that during the clashes that had occurred earlier in Kibuye préfecture, Tutsi civilians had taken refuge in churches[24] and, on the other hand, that between 8 and 15 April 1994, thousands of Tutsi civilians sought shelter in Mubuga church.[25] He admits that the Tutsi who had assembled at the church had been attacked between 14 and 17 April 1994,[26] and that, as a result, thousands of men, women and children who had gathered there died or were wounded.[27] Prior to the attack, the Accused had observed the attackers, including the bourgmestre, armed Hutu civilians, commune policemen and members of the national gendarmerie assembling.[28]

33. Despite his position and of his having knowledge of the above-mentioned events, the Accused failed to act to protect the Tutsi, either before or after the massacres.[29] Witness TRV- 4

[21] Guilty Plea Agreement, para. 19.
[22] Ibid., para. 20.
[23] Ibid., para. 21.
[24] Ibid., para. 23.
[25] Ibid., para. 22.
[26] Ibid., para. 24.
[27] Ibid., para. 27.
[28] Ibid., para. 26.
[29] Ibid., para. 29.

34. During the hearing of 17 January 2005, Witness TRV-4, a Tutsi woman, who had known the Accused since 1985, testified that the Accused had saved her life[30] during the events of 1994 when she lost 35 members of her family.[31] She explained that Vincent Rutaganira had some Tutsi friends, and that his friendship with them was symbolized by mutual gifts of cows and joint celebration of marriages. TRV-4 testified that she had gone into hiding during the events of 1994 and had been discovered by attackers. She had then produced a false Hutu identity card, before being taken by the attackers to a place where other attackers were getting ready to go and kill people in Bisesero. Vincent Rutaganira was at that place. When the attackers tried to kill her, Vincent Rutaganira intervened, saying that her identity card showed that she was Hutu. The attackers said that if they did not kill her, Vincent Rutaganira had to give them one of her children for them to kill instead. The attackers then dispersed.[32]

Immaculée Nyiramasimbi

35. Known under the pseudonym KNN 1, Immaculée Nyiramasimbi, a Defence witness, sought and obtained leave of the Chamber not to testify under a pseudonym.[33] Immaculée Nyiramasimbi has been married to the Accused since 1973 and they bore nine children. She is currently deputy mayor in charge of women's development in her commune.[34]

36. Immaculée Nyiramasimbi testified that Vincent Rutaganira became conseiller communal for Mubuga secteur because the people had a great deal of confidence in him and he worked in close collaboration with them. While in office, he had restored security in Mubuga secteur by putting an end to

30 T.17 January 2005, p. 20.
31 Ibid., p. 19.
32 Ibid., p. 20: "In a pre-trial statement, TRV-4 had stated that she was attacked around 20 April at Ryaruhanga centre."
33 Ibid., p. 22.
34 Ibid., p. 23.

the activities of criminals who used to attack and rob people. At the time, the Accused was in good terms with the Tutsi as reflected in mutual gifts of cows and participation in weddings. Mr. Rutaganira and his wife had Tutsi godchildren and had chosen Tutsi as godfathers and godmothers to their own children.[35] They get on well with the survivors.[36]

37. The witness also testified that Vincent Rutaganira did not get on well with the bourgmestre before and during the events of April 1994, especially since the Accused did not wish to participate in the massacres. She added that she and her husband had been threatened during that period.[37]

38. The witness further testified that she and the Accused had agreed to hide Tutsis at home during the events of 1994 and specifically that some Tutsi girls and a Tutsi woman had stayed at their house for two weeks and three months respectively. She asserted that nobody had died or been wounded at the roadblock that had been erected near their house, and that no property had been looted.[38]

Witness KPP 1

39. Witness KPP 1 testified that he had been detained for eight years[39] and that, being a widower, he remarried a survivor.[40]

40. KPP 1 certified that he knew the Accused before the events of 1994. He testified that when the Accused was conseiller communal, he had restored security in the secteur, which had previously been disrupted by bandits and hooligans who used to steal from and attack the people. KPP 1 added that the people were grateful to the Accused for saving them from the bandit attacks.[41]

---

[35] T.17 January 2005, p. 24.
[36] Ibid., p. 26.
[37] Idem.
[38] Idem.
[39] Ibid., p. 29.
[40] Ibid., p. 31.
[41] Ibid., p. 29.

According to the witness, the Accused as conseiller de secteur, had taken many decisions in the public's interest and against the interests of his friends.[42] He stated that Vincent Rutaganira had been on good terms with the Tutsi; that he is a godfather to their children, just as some Tutsi are godfathers to his children. KPP 1 testified that Vincent Rutaganira did not get on well with the bourgmestre.[43]

41. KPP 1 testified that had Vincent Rutaganira been fully in charge during the events of 1994, he would have taken action against the bandits, hooligans and armed gangsters who had taken control of the situation.[44]

Witness TRV-6

42. The Defense submitted to the Chamber a statement from Witness TRV-6 dated 21 January 2003.[45] The witness, whose entire family was killed during the genocide, testified that two days after the death of President Habyarimana, she sought refuge at the Accused's house, and subsequently in another house belonging to him, where she remained for over three months. She was supported by the Accused during her stay in his house.

43. On two occasions, Witness TRV-6 had heard the bourgmestre invite the Accused to join him in attacks but the Accused had refused and also denied that he had hidden some Tutsi.

Witness TRV-9

44. The Defense submitted to the Chamber a statement dated 21 January 2003 from Witness TRV-9,[46] whose family and that of Accused Vincent Rutaganira were friends. TRV- 9 testified that only three members of his

---

[42] Ibid., p. 30.
[43] T.17 January 2005, p. 30.
[44] Ibid., p. 31.
[45] Exhibit D1. 2D.
[46] Exhibit D1. 3D.

family had survived the genocide. He explained that during the events of 7 April 1994, his children had been saved and protected by the Accused in his house. TRV-9 stated that the Accused had been able to save many Tutsi because they trusted him. He added that before the war, the people already knew that Vincent Rutaganira did not get on well with the bourgmestre.

Witness TRV-10

45. The Defence submitted to the Chamber a statement from Witness TRV-10, dated 23 January 2003.[47] TRV-10 testified, inter alia, that during the events of 1994, she had been taken to the Accused's house after being raped. The Accused reassured her by telling her not to be afraid. She added that when the bourgmestre arrived at the Accused's house, the Accused told the bourgmestre that she was a Hutu. The bourgmestre therefore asked the Accused to help her. The Accused then took her to the dispensary and gave orders that she not be harmed.

[47] Exhibit D1. 4D.

CHAPTER IV:

CRIMINAL RESPONSIBILITY OF THE ACCUSED ON THE COUNT OF EXTERMINATION AS A CRIME AGAINST HUMANITY (COUNT 16 OF THE INDICTMENT)

46. Chapter VI of the Indictment of the guilty plea agreement reads: "[In the light of the points of fact and law set forth in this agreement and acknowledged by the Accused, there is no doubt that Vincent Rutaganira, by omission and as an accomplice, aided and abetted the commission of the crime of extermination as a crime against humanity within the meaning of Article 6(1) of the Statute]".

47. The crime to which the Accused pleaded guilty is covered under Article 3(b) with the form of participation being provided under Article 6(1) of the Statute. Under Rule 62(B)(iv), in determining the Accused's responsibility for the crime to which he pleaded guilty, the Chamber must not only satisfy itself that all the elements of the crime of extermination are present, but also ascertain the form of Vincent Rutaganira's participation in the perpetration of the said crime.

A. *Extermination as a crime against humanity (Article 3(b) of the Statute of the Tribunal)*

48. With respect to crimes against humanity, Article 3(b) of the Statute provides that the Tribunal shall have the power to prosecute persons responsible for the crime of extermination:

- when the crime was committed as part of a widespread or systematic attack against any civilian population, and
- where the civilian population was the target of such an attack on national, political, ethnic, racial or religious grounds.

1. The massacres at Mubuga church between 14 and 17 April 1994

49. Nahimana et al. held that "in order to be guilty of the crime of extermination, the Accused must have been involved in killings of civilians on a large scale".[48] Akayesu ruled that extermination "is a crime which by its very nature is directed against a group of individuals [and] differs from murder in that it requires an element of mass destruction".[49] In Bagilishema, the Trial Chamber found that "extermination is unlawful killing on a large scale", and that "large scale" does not suggest a numerical minimum. It must be determined on a case-by-case basis using a common-sense approach".[50]

50. Therefore, the Chamber notes that the Tribunal has consistently held that, by its very nature, extermination is a crime which is directed against a group of individuals as distinct from murder in that it must be perpetrated on a "large scale."

[48] Nahimana et al. Judgement (TC), para. 1061.
[49] Akayesu Judgement (TC), para. 591. The Trial Chamber adopted the same definition in Kayishema and Ruzindana Judgement (TC), para. 145 and in Rutaganda Judgement (TC), para. 82. See also Musema Judgement (TC), para. 217, Ntakirutimana Judgement (TC), para. 813 and Semanza Judgement (TC), para. 259;
[50] Bagilishema Judgement (TC), para. 87.

51. In his guilty plea, Vincent Rutaganira admits that the attackers who surrounded and attacked Mubuga church between 14 and 17 April 1994 included representatives of the local authorities, armed Hutu civilians, commune policemen and members of the gendarmerie. The Accused also admits that thousands of refugees were killed or wounded at Mubuga church massacres perpetrated during the same period.

52. It has also been established that the attacks perpetrated in Kibuye préfecture, including those perpetrated between l4 and 17 April 1994 at Mubuga church against the Tutsi people, led to mass killings on a large scale.[51]

53. Therefore, the Chamber finds that the massacres committed at Mubuga church between 14 and 17 April 1994 had been perpetrated on a large scale and had caused thousands of casualties.

2. Widespread and systematic attack

54. That massacres had been perpetrated at Mubuga church between 15 and 17 April 1994 as part of a widespread and systematic attack was indisputably admitted by the Accused Vincent Rutaganira in his guilty plea, under chapters V and VI of the Agreement.

55. It has also been shown with respect to the events which took place in Kibuye prefecture, that large scale killings had been perpetrated at Mubuga church during the same period as admitted by the Accused in his guilty plea agreement, and that such killings had been part of a widespread and systematic attack in said préfecture.[52]

56. The Chamber finds that the facts in the instant case are sufficient to prove beyond a reasonable doubt that massacres were perpetrated at Mubuga church between 14 and 17 April 1994, as part of a widespread and systematic attack.

[51] Kayishema and Ruzindana Judgement (TC), paras. 317 and 404.
[52] Kayishema and Ruzindana Judgement (TC), para. 576.

3. The civilian population targeted on ethnic grounds

57. In his guilty plea, the Accused Vincent Rutaganira admits that between 8 and 15 April 994, thousands of Tutsi civilians – men, women and children – had sought refuge at Mubuga church in Mubuga secteur (Gishyita commune), from attacks that had been launched against them. The Accused also admits that those people were victims of the abovementioned massacres because they were members of the Tutsi ethnic group.

58. It has also been shown that the victims of the attack at Mubuga church between 14 and 17 April 1994 were mainly members of the Tutsi ethnic group.[53]

59. In the opinion of the Chamber, it has been shown that the widespread and systematic attack during which the Mubuga church massacres took place during the relevant period, had been perpetrated against a civilian population on ethnic grounds.

60. Accordingly, the Chamber finds that such massacres amount to extermination under Article 3(b) of the Statute.

B. Participation of the Accused Vincent Rutaganira in the crime of extermination (crime against humanity) through complicity by omission

61. The Accused pleaded guilty of the crime of extermination as a crime against humanity (Count 16 of the Indictment), through complicity by omission.

62. It is the case that complicity is not expressly included among the forms of liability enumerated in Article 6(1), which provides:

A person who planned, instigated, ordered, committed or otherwise

[53] Idem.

aided and abetted in the planning, preparation or execution of a crime referred to in Articles 2 to 4 of the present Statute, shall be individually responsible for the crime.

63. The case-law of both ad hoc Tribunals has indeed determined a form of complicity in aiding and abetting provided for under Article 6(1). Thus, in Furundžija, an ICTY Trial Chamber held that complicity "consists of practical assistance, encouragement, or moral support which has a substantial effect on the perpetration of the crime".[54]

64. The Chamber must also satisfy itself that aiding and abetting as provided for in Article 6(1) can be constituted by an omission and not only by an act. For instance, in Blaškić, the ICTY Trial Chamber held that "the actus reus of aiding and abetting may be perpetrated through an omission, provided this failure to act had a decisive effect on the commission of the crime and that it was coupled with the requisite mens rea".[55] In Rutaganda, the Trial Chamber of the Tribunal held that "an accused may participate in the commission of a crime either through direct commission of an unlawful act or by omission, where he has a duty to act".[56]

65. Accordingly, the Chamber finds that participation by omission in extermination as a crime against humanity as admitted to by the Accused Vincent Rutaganira is covered under Article 6(1) of the Statute.

66. The Chamber must therefore consider the elements of aiding and abetting by omission, namely, the act (actus reus) and the mental element (mens rea).

[54] Furundžija Judgement (TC), paras. 235 and 249.
[55] Blaškić Judgement (TC), paras. 284.
[56] Rutaganda Judgement (TC), para. 41.

1. Actus reus

67. The Chamber notes that determining omission under Article 6(1) of the Statute is a more complex task than showing omission under Article 6(3). In the latter case, omission can be attributed to a person who, de jure and/or de facto, has an unambiguous status as a military or civilian superior. Such is not the case under Article 6(1) in the instant case.

68. In determining participation by omission in extermination as a crime against humanity as admitted to by the Accused, the Chamber addressed the following questions:

(i) Did the Accused have authority and did he choose to not exercise it?

(ii) Did the Accused have a moral authority over the principals such as to prevent them from committing the crime and did he choose not to exercise it?

(iii) Was the Accused under a legal duty to act which he failed to fulfill?

(i) Powers vested in the conseiller communal, Vincent Rutaganira, under the relevant statutory provisions

69. Regarding the Accused's power to act, the Chamber recalls that Vincent Rutaganira did mention his position as conseiller communal for Mubuga secteur (Gishyita commune, Kibuye préfecture) during the events that occurred at Mubuga church, as reflected in the guilty plea agreement. Vincent Rutaganira was, inter alia, in charge of economic, social and cultural issues in his secteur.[57] He also admitted that he was "[the link between all the inhabitants of Mubuga secteur and the local political structure, within the limits of his duties under the Organic Law of November 1963]".[58] Lastly, he admitted that although he was conseiller of Mubuga secteur, he had not acted to protect the Tutsi who sought refuge at Mubuga church between 8 and 15 April 1994.[59]

[57] Guilty Plea Agreement, para. 29.
[58] Ibid., para. 21; Article 37 of the Law of 23 November 1963 on Communal Organization.
[59] Ibid., para. 29.

CIII05-0020 (E)
Translation certified by LSS, ICTR

70. The Chamber notes that under Article 37 of the Rwandan law on communal organization,[60] the position of conseiller communal for his secteur conferred on the Accused authority to chair public meetings in Mubuga secteur and to note and convey the wishes of the people. Such authority implies the power to convene such meetings and to draw up agendas therefor.

71. The Chamber recalls that Witness KPP 1 testified that before the events of 1994, the Accused Vincent Rutaganira, while in office, had managed to restore security in Mubuga secteur which had hitherto experienced growing insecurity caused by bandits and hooligans who used to steal and attack the people. The testimony of KPP 1 was also corroborated by Witness Immaculée Nyiramasimbi. Moreover, several testimonies[61] showed that out of his sense of justice, Vincent Rutaganira readily opposed any decisions by the bourgmestre of Gishyita commune, Charles Sikubwabo, which struck him as unfair to or inappropriate for the people in the secteur, with his relations with the bourgmestre being strained as a result.

72. Therefore, the Chamber finds that the Accused had the power to convene a meeting of the inhabitants of the secteur to initiate and conduct discussions on the tragic events that were taking place in his secteur, in order to prevent participation in the massacres that occurred at the church, at least, by civilians. The Chamber notes in this regard that, according to the guilty plea agreement, armed Hutu civilians, commune policemen and members of the gendarmerie, who were joined by civilians, perpetrated attacks.

73. The Chamber finds that the Accused's admission that he did not attempt to prevent the attacks on the Tutsi although he was conseiller of Mubugu secteur amounted to an implicit admission that he presumably had the power to do so.

---

[60] Law of 23 November 1963 on Communal Organisation (Official Gazette, 1963, p. 507), amended by Legislative Decree of 26 September 1974 (Official Gazette, 1974, p. 577) and Legislative Decree No. 4/75 of 30 January 1975 (Official Gazette,1975, p. 191).

[61] Exhibits D1. 1D and D1. 3D.

74. Therefore, the Chamber finds that as conseiller de secteur with definite, albeit limited powers, the Accused Vincent Rutaganira chose to not exercise such powers during the events that occurred in Mubuga between 14 and 17 April 1994. He particularly failed to take action against the civilians who had joined the armed attackers to kill Tutsi refugees at Mubuga church.

(ii) The Accused's moral authority in Mubuga secteur during the events

75. As regards the Accused's moral authority, the Chamber recalls that in the Guilty Plea Agreement, the Accused acknowledged that "[he was a prominent member of the community in Mubuga secteur (Gishyita commune)]" and that he "[was the closest personality to the people at the secteur level]".[62]

76. The Chamber also notes that the evidence clearly shows that at the time of the April 1994 events in Rwanda, the people of Mubuga had total confidence in Vincent Rutaganira because of his position as conseiller communal for his secteur and his good reputation as a fair and courageous man. Witness KPP 1 testified inter alia that the people felt particularly grateful to the Accused for restoring security in the secteur, which had previously been disrupted by bandits. Witness TRV-4 testified that Vincent Rutaganira had saved his life and had been quick to intervene when the attackers tried to kill him after surprising him in his hideout. Witness TRV-4 also gave a detailed account of how the Accused came out of his shop for the express purpose of assisting him when he was under threat from the attackers. The Accused's moral authority over the inhabitants of the secteur is also reflected in the testimony of Witness Immaculée Nyiramasimbi, who testified that nobody died or was wounded at the roadblock that had been erected near the Accused's house, unlike at the other roadblocks erected during the said events.

77. Therefore, the Chamber finds that the Accused Vincent Rutaganira, who was conseiller communal for Mubuga secteur for 10 years, still enjoyed moral authority over the population of the said secteur as a whole during the

[62] Guilty Plea Agreement, para. 21.

events that occurred at Mubuga church between 14 and 17 April 1994. Thus, he could have used his moral authority to prevent some members of the public from participating in the attacks at the church, as he had done by protecting some Tutsi from attackers near his shop.

(iii) Legal duties placed on the Accused Vincent Rutaganira

78. The Chamber wishes to add, ad abundantiam, that international law also places upon a person vested with public authority a duty to act in order to protect human life. Indeed, the State to which it falls to carry out international obligations, can only act through all its representatives, be they in the upper reaches or at lower levels of Government. The State itself can fulfil its international obligations and not incur any responsibility not only because of its representatives' respect for human rights but also by reason of actions taken, in the performance of their duties, to prevent any violation of the said rights.[63] Hence, the need to incorporate international standards in municipal law, as provided for by all relevant international agreements. The State of Rwandan did so, in particular, with respect to the standards set forth in international human rights instruments, international humanitarian law and respecting individual criminal responsibility for crimes against humanity and war crimes.[64]

79. Consequently, as any person, all public authorities have a duty not only to comply with the basic rights of the human person, but also to ensure that these are complied with,[65] which implies a duty to act in order to prevent any violation of such rights.

[63] See also the commitment under Article 4(c) of the International Convention on the Elimination of All Forms of Racial Discrimination, also incorporated in Rwandan law (Legislative Decree No. 08/75 of 12 February 1975, Official Gazette, 1975, p. 230) "Shall not permit public authorities or public institutions, national or local, to promote or incite racial discrimination." "Article II of the Convention on the Non-Applicability of Statutory Limitations to War Crimes and Crimes Against Humanity."

[64] Not only have all these international conventions been incorporated into Rwandan domestic law upon their being published in the Official Gazette following ratification, but the basic rights of the human person are also enshrined in Articles 12 to 33 of the Constitution in force in 1994. The Arusha Peace Accords, which were also incorporated into the Rwandan Constitution also provided for such obligations.

[65] The obligation in question is explicitly set forth in, for example, Article 1 Common to the Geneva Conventions.

80. The Chamber notes that in assessing the Accused's culpable conduct under Article 6(1) of the Statute, the Defence submitted in its closing arguments at the hearing of 17 January 2005, that the Accused had shirked his legal duty to humanity. More specifically, the Defence made reference to the fact that every Rwandan citizen who fails to provide assistance to a person in danger could be held criminally responsible.[66]

81. In the opinion of the Chamber, while under the so called "[risk to oneself and to another]" doctrine set forth in Article 256 of the Rwandan Penal Code a person may justifiably fail to act, such a doctrine may not provide complete exoneration in light of the particularly serious nature of the crimes committed during the events that occurred in Rwanda in 1994. Indeed, violence to physical well-being suffered by thousands of people during the said events affects the very fundamental interests of Humanity as a whole, and the protection of such interests cannot be counterbalanced by the mere personal risk that may have been faced by any person in a position of authority who failed to act in order to assist people whose lives were in danger.[67]

82. In the instant, by reason of the authority vested in him by virtue of his office the Accused Vincent Rutaganira was under a duty to provide assistance to people in danger, pursuant to Article 256 of the Rwandan Penal Code.

83. Lastly, the Chamber notes that because of his unique position, the Accused had a duty to report to the relevant authorities the crimes that were being committed against the Tutsi population in his secteur.

84. Accordingly, the Chamber finds that the Accused Vincent Rutaganira had a duty to prevent some inhabitants in his secteur from participating in attacks against the civilians who had taken refuge at Mubuga church, to provide such civilians with assistance and to report the attackers to the relevant authorities, but chose not to do so.

[66] Article 256 paras. 1 and 2 of the Rwandan Penal Code, Legislative Decree No. 21/77 of 18 August 1977 (version in force in 1994).

[67] Erdemović Judgement, (TC), para. 19: "With regard to a crime against humanity, the Trial Chamber considers that the life of the accused and that of the victim are not fully equivalent. As opposed to ordinary law, the violation here is no longer directed at the physical welfare of the victim alone but at humanity as a whole."

(iv) Connection between the perpetration of the crime and participation by aiding and abetting

(a) Temporal and geographical connection

85. Under the case-law of the ad hoc Tribunals, there must be a temporal and geographical connection between criminal participation under Article 6(1) and the perpetration of the crime.[68] Furthermore, participation may occur before, during or after the act is committed and be geographically separated therefrom.[69]

86. In the instant case, Vincent Rutaganira stood a few metres away from the place where the attackers assembled before and after the attacks. Thus, he was in a position to observe them as they assembled near his house and subsequently to know that attacks were being perpetrated on Mubuga church, between 14 and 17 April 1994.

87. Therefore, the Chamber finds that Vincent Rutaganira participated by omission in extermination as a crime against humanity both before and during the massacre of refugees perpetrated at Mubuga church.

(b) Effect of aiding and abetting on the perpetration of a crime by the principal perpetrator

88. Both ad hoc Tribunals have held that for criminal responsibility under Article 6(1) to attach, the act of aiding and abetting must have a decisive[70] and substantial effect[71] on the commission of the crime by the principal perpetrator.

[68] Furundžija Judgement (TC), para. 234 ; Aleksovski Judgement (TC), para. 129; Blaškić Judgement (AC), para. 47.
[69] Blaškić Judgement (TC), para. 285.
[70] Ibid., (AC), para. 284.
[71] Rutaganda Judgement (AC), para. 43; Musema Judgement (AC), para. 126; Bagilishema Judgement (AC), para. 33; Ntakirutimana Judgement (AC), para. 787.

89. In the light of such case-law, the Chamber is of the opinion that for an accused to incur criminal responsibility under Article 6(1) of the Statute, it must be shown that his or her participation has substantially contributed to, or has had a substantial effect on the consummation of a crime under the Statute. With respect to aiding and abetting by omission, such contribution or effect can be assessed only against the effectiveness of any action taken to prevent the commission of the crime.

90. The Chamber finds that in the instant case, Vincent Rutaganira's intervention saved some people who had been targeted by attackers. It can be inferred from such a finding that a similar intervention by the Accused against some civilians who participated in the attacks on Mubuga church would have had the same decisive effect in sparing human lives.

91. On the basis of objective indicia and the lack of any material disagreement between the Prosecutor and the Accused, the Chamber is satisfied that the facts admitted by the Accused are quite sufficient to prove the existence of the actus reus of aiding and abetting by omission, extermination as a crime against humanity as committed by the attackers on Mubuga church between 14 and 17 April 1994.

2. Mens rea

92. Pursuant to the case-law of the Tribunal[72] and of ICTY,[73] the Chamber is of the opinion that the mens rea of an accomplice lies in his knowledge of, on the one hand, the mens rea of the principal perpetrator of the crime and, on the other hand, of the fact that his conduct would further the perpetration of the crime.

[72] Akayesu Judgement (AC), para. 539; Musema Judgement (TC), para. 181.
[73] Vasiljevic Judgement (AC), para. 102; Blaškić Judgement (AC), para. 45.

93. The Chamber must determine whether the Accused Vincent Rutaganira had knowledge:

(i) of the principal perpetrator committing extermination as part of a widespread and systematic attack against a civilian population on ethnic grounds; and

(ii) of his own conduct furthering the perpetration of said crime

94. In determining whether the Accused had the mens rea of the crime admitted, the Chamber will rely on Vincent Rutaganira's confessions and some objective indicia.

(i) Knowledge of extermination perpetrated as part of a widespread and systematic attack against a civilian population on ethnic grounds

95. The Chamber finds that, as reflected in the guilty plea agreement, the Accused knew that between 8 and 15 April 1994, thousands of Tutsi civilians had sought refuge at Mubuga church, in Mubuga secteur (Gishyita commune) from attacks targeting their ethnic group.[74] Vincent Rutaganira admits that the attack on the Tutsi civilians who had assembled in Mubuga church was part of a widespread and systematic attack.[75] Indeed, the Chamber notes that, by virtue of his position as conseiller communal for Mubuga secteur, the Accused must have known about the serious events that were occurring in his secteur and the crimes that were being perpetrated there on a large scale.

96. In the light of the above the Chamber finds that the Accused knew about the general context in which the massacres were being perpetrated at Mubuga church during the relevant period, namely that his omissions were part of a widespread and systematic attack targeted at the civilian population on ethnic grounds.

(ii) Knowledge that his conduct furthered the principal perpetrator's crime

[74] Guilty plea agreement, para. 22.

[75] Ibid., para. 30.

97. The Chamber finds that Vincent Rutaganira was aware not only of his duties as conseiller communal for Mubuga secteur but also of his moral authority vis à vis the civilian population in his secteur. Indeed, Vincent Rutaganira admits that "[although he was conseiller of Mubuga secteur, he did not act to protect the Tutsis who had sheltered at Mubuga church in Mubuga secteur (Gishyita commune) between 8 and 15 April 1994]".[76]

98. Accordingly, the Chamber finds that the Accused was aware that his failure to act would further the commission of the crime.

99. As a result, the Chamber finds that the Accused knew that his omissions would further the commission of the crime.

C. Findings

100. In light of the foregoing, the Chamber finds that there is sufficient evidence to prove that the Accused Vincent Rutaganira is guilty of extermination as a crime against humanity as charged in count 16 of the Indictment, in that he aided and abetted by omission the commission of the said crime.

[76] Ibid., para. 29.

CHAPTER V:

INDIVIDUAL CRIMINAL RESPONSIBILITY OF THE ACCUSED ON COUNTS 1, 14, 15, 17, 18 AND 19

A. Submissions of the Parties

101. In the Indictment of 6 May 1996, in addition to Count 16, the Prosecutor charged Vincent Rutaganira with the following counts:

(i) Count 1: Conspiracy to commit genocide, under Article 2(3)(a) of the Statute of the Tribunal.
(ii) Count 14: Genocide, under Article 2(3)(a) of the Statute of the Tribunal.
(iii) Count 17: Crimes against humanity (murder), under Article 3(a) of the Statute of the Tribunal.
(iv) Count 17: Crimes against humanity (other inhumane acts), under Article 3(i) of the Statute of the Tribunal.
(v) Count 18: Violation of Article 3 common to the Geneva Conventions, under Article 4(a) of the Statute of the Tribunal.
(vi) Count 19: Violation of Additional Protocol II to the Geneva Conventions, under Article 4(a) of the Statute of the Tribunal.

102. During his appearance at the hearing of 8 December 2004, the Accused Vincent Rutaganira pleaded not guilty to Counts 1, 14, 15, 17, 18 and 19.

103. At the hearing of 17 January 2005, citing a lack of evidence to support its allegations, the Prosecution reiterated its request made at the hearing of 8 December 2004 that Counts 1, 14, 15, 17, 18 and 19 be dismissed and that the Accused be acquitted on said counts.

B. Findings

104. Having ascertained the will of the parties, the Chamber notes that where there is an agreement between the parties, the Accused may sometimes be required as a result to waive his right to be presumed innocent, thereby relieving the Prosecution of the burden of proving guilt beyond a reasonable doubt at trial. It follows that, if, as in the instant case, the Prosecution concedes that it lacks evidence to support its allegations, in the absence of any other judicially noticed facts or facts proving the responsibility of the Accused, the Chamber, being responsible for ensuring a fair trial and compliance with the rights of the Accused, is in a position to find, on the evidence before it, that there is no basis for convicting Vincent Rutaganira on Counts 1, 14, 15, 17, 18 and 19.

CHAPTER VI: VERDICT

105. The Chamber finds Vincent Rutaganira:

- Count 1: Conspiracy to commit genocide, under Article 2(3)(b) of the Statute of the Tribunal: NOT GUILTY

- Count 14: Genocide, under Article 2(3)(a) of the Statute: NOT GUILTY

- Count 15: crimes against humanity (murder), under Article 3(a) of the Statute of the Tribunal: NOT GUILTY

- Count 16: crimes against humanity (extermination), under Article 3(b) of the Statute of the Tribunal: GUILTY

- Count 17: Crimes against humanity (other inhumane act), under Article 3(i) of the Statute of the Tribunal: NOT GUILTY;

- Count 18: Violation of Article 3 common to the Geneva Convention, under Article 4(a) of the Statute of the Tribunal: NOT GUILTY;

- Count 19: Violation of Additional Protocol II of the Geneva Conventions, under Article 4(a) of the Statute of the Tribunal: NOT GUILTY.

CHAPTER VII:

DETERMINATION OF SENTENCE

A. Sentencing principles

106. Neither the Statute nor the Rules provide explicitly for the penalties applicable to the various crimes within the jurisdiction of the Tribunal. Therefore, in determining appropriate sentences within the guidelines set by the provisions of the Statute and Rules, the Chamber has discretion as to the factors to be taken into account. The relevant provisions relating to sentencing are as follows:

Article 23 of the Statute
Penalties

> 1. The penalty imposed by the Trial Chamber shall be limited to imprisonment. In determining the terms of imprisonment, the Trial Chambers shall have recourse to the general practice regarding prison sentences in the courts of Rwanda.
>
> 2. In imposing the sentences, the Trial Chambers should take into account such factors as the gravity of the offence and the individual circumstances of the convicted person.
>
> 3. In addition to imprisonment, the Trial Chambers may order the return of any property and proceeds acquired by criminal conduct, including by means of duress, to their rightful owners.

Rule 100 of the Rules

Sentencing Procedure on a Guilty Plea

(A) If the Trial Chamber convicts the accused on a guilty plea, the Prosecutor and the Defence may submit any relevant information that may assist the Trial Chamber in determining an appropriate sentence.
[...]

Rule 101: Penalties

(A) A person convicted by the Tribunal may be sentenced to imprisonment for a fixed term or the remainder of his life.

(B) In determining the sentence, the Trial Chamber shall take into account the factors mentioned in Article 23 (2) of the Statute, as well as such factors as:

(i) Any aggravating circumstances;
(ii) Any mitigating circumstances including the substantial cooperation with the Prosecutor by the convicted person before or after conviction;
(iii) The general practice regarding prison sentences in the courts of Rwanda;
[...]

(C) The Trial Chamber shall indicate whether multiple sentences shall be served consecutively or concurrently.

(D) Credit shall be given to the convicted person for the period, if any, during which the convicted person was detained in custody pending his surrender to the Tribunal or pending trial or appeal.

107. The Chamber shall determine Vincent Rutaganira's sentence in compliance with the provisions of Article 23 of the Statute, Rules 100 and 101 of the Rules and the case-law of the Tribunal which identifies retribution, deterrence and rehabilitation as the main purposes of a punishment.

108. Retribution is the expression of the social disapproval attached to a criminal act and to its perpetrator and demands punishment for the latter for what he has done. The sentences handed down by the International Criminal Tribunal are therefore an expression of humanity's outrage against the serious violations of human rights and international humanitarian law which an accused has been found guilty of committing.[77] Retribution meets the need for justice and may also appease the anger caused by the crime to the victims and within the community as a whole.

109. In citing retribution as a major purpose of the sentence, the Chamber underscores the gravity of the crime to which the Accused has pleaded guilty, given the specific circumstances of the instant case.

110. With the sentence, an attempt is made to deter, that is, to discourage people from committing similar crimes.[78] The main result sought is to discourage people from committing a second offence (special deterrence) since the penalty should also result in discouraging other people from carrying out their criminal plans (general deterrence).[79]

111. The Chamber shall assess the factors relevant to « special deterrence » in considering circumstances in mitigation.

112. With respect to general deterrence, a sentence would contribute to strengthening the legal system which criminalizes the conduct charged and to assuring society that its criminal system is effective.

113. By « rehabilitation », the Chamber understands the need to take into account the ability of the person found guilty to be rehabilitated; such rehabilitation goes hand in hand with his reintegration into society.[80]

---

[77] Aleksovski Judgement, (AC) para. 185.
[78] Todorović Judgement (TC), para. 30.
[79] Tadić Judgement (TC), paras. 7-9.
[80] Čelebići Judgement (AC), para. 806; Banović Judgement (TC), para. 35.

114. In the opinion of the Chamber, when an accused pleads guilty, he is taking an important step towards rehabilitation and reintegration.[81] Such admission of guilt is likely to contribute to the search for the truth; it shows the resolve of an accused to accept responsibility vis-à-vis the injured party and society as a whole, which may contribute to reconciliation which is one of the goals pursued by the Tribunal.

B. Factors to be taken into account

115. In determining a sentence, the Chamber must take the following factors into account: the gravity of the offence, the individual circumstances of the accused, any aggravating and mitigating circumstances and the general practice regarding prison sentences in the courts of Rwanda.

1. Gravity of the crime

(i) Prosecution's submissions

116. The Prosecution prayed the Chamber to take into account the gravity of the crime when determining sentence. In particular, it submitted that the crime to which the Accused pleaded guilty constitutes a crime «of extreme gravity, the scale of which shock collective conscience».[82]

(ii) Discussion

117. In the opinion of the Chamber, the gravity of the criminal conduct is the primary factor to be taken into account when sentencing. In Čelebići, the Appeals Chamber endorsed « the principle that the gravity of the offence is the primary consideration in imposing sentence».[83] It also held that "the

[81] NikolićJudgement (TC), para. 93.
[82] T.17 January 2005, p. 5.
[83] Čelebići Judgement (AC), para. 731: Todorović Judgement (AC), para. 31.

determination of the gravity of the crime requires a consideration of the particular circumstances of the case, as well as the form and degree of the participation of the accused in the crime".[84]

118. Vincent Rutaganira admitted to having aided and abetted, as an accomplice by omission, the extermination of thousands of civilian refugees at Mubuga church in April 1994. Such acts of extermination constitute a crime against humanity under Article 3 of the Statute and, as such, constitute serious outrages upon personal dignity.

119. It is the Chamber's view that the gravity of the crime charged is to be assessed in relation to the degree of the Accused's participation in the crime. In that regard, it should be noted that Vincent Rutaganira did not participate actively in the killings at Mubuga church. However, since he failed to act to prevent such killings, he was found guilty of having aided and abetted the massacres.

2. Individual circumstance

2.1 Family circumstance

(i) Submissions of the parties

120. As testified to in open session by the Accused and his wife, nine children were born of their union. Moreover, his wife testified that she serves in the new Government as deputy mayor in charge of women's development in her commune.[85] This evidence was not disputed by the Prosecutor.

---

[84] Čelebići Judgement (AC), para. 731.
[85] T.18 January 2004, p. 26.

(ii) Discussion

121. The Chamber is of the view that such evidence augurs well for the potential rehabilitation of the Accused into the local community and his joining the national reconciliation process.[86]

2.2 Personality and general conduct of the Accused

(i) Submission of the parties and evidence

122. It is undisputed that prior to the events in the instant, Vincent Rutaganira was a man of upstanding character who placed the public interest over his personal interest[87] and that his sense of duty and presence during the events of 1994 enabled him to save lives.[88]

123. Witness TRV-4 testified about the good relationship the Accused maintained with the Tutsi in the following terms: "Yes, he was a friend of the Tutsis, and I say that because he exchanged cattle with the Tutsis. He went to their weddings; their families went to each other's weddings"[89]. This evidence was confirmed by Witness Immaculée Nyiramasimbi,[90] the wife of the Accused who explained that Vincent Rutaganira is godfather to Tutsi children who are still alive. The witness further testified that the Accused also exchanged cows with more than 10 families, explaining that in Rwandan culture, such exchange of cows is a "symbol of love, faithfulness, and cooperation".[91]

124. Immaculée Nyiramasimbi testified further that in his capacity as conseiller of Mubuga secteur, Vincent Rutaganira had restored security and that "the population trusted him a great deal".[92] Immaculée Nyiramasimbi

[86] Joint Brief paras. 25-26.
[87] Ibid., para. 33.
[88] Ibid., para. 34.
[89] T.17 January 2005, p. 16.
[90] Initially, this witness bore the pseudonym KNN1. At the hearing, just before he began her testimony, she sought permission from the Chamber to testify in open court without protection. See T.17 January 2005, p. 17.
[91] T.17 January 2005, p. 20. See also testimony of KPP1, p. 30.
[92] T.17 January 2005, p. 19.

explained that by restoring peace and order in the secteur, Vincent Rutaganira earned some enemies.[93] The witness also testified about actions taken by the Accused in his capacity as conseiller: he managed to ensure water supply for his secteur, the health centre, the primary school, the trading centre and the cellules.[94]

125. Moreover, Witness KKP 1 testified about a personal experience during which his friend Vincent Rutaganira decided to expropriate his plot of land in order to use it to supply water to Mubuga secteur, thereby causing the population's interest to prevail over that of a friend. Witness KKP 1 went on to state that: "So, I needed time to understand exactly what he was doing to me, and I understood that he was doing that because he was an upright citizen acting on behalf of the population. I understood that".[95]

(ii) Discussion

126. The Prosecutor did not challenge any of the witnesses called by Defence.

127. The Chamber will consider the personality and general conduct of the Accused in determining his sentence.

2.3 Lack of a criminal record and good conduct while in detention

(i) Submissions of the parties

128. Both parties cited Vincent Rutaganira's lack of a criminal record and good conduct since being remanded in custody at the United Nations Detention Facility in Arusha. The Defence tendered a good conduct certificate issued by officials of the Facility.[96]

---

[93] Ibid., p. 24.
[94] Ibid., p. 20.
[95] Ibid., p. 24.
[96] Joint Brief, para. 35; T.17 January 2005, p. 39. Exhibit No. D4 (sealed).

(ii) Discussion

129. The Chamber notes that the ICTY viewed the lack of criminal convictions as a mitigating circumstance[97] as it did the comportment and behaviour of the Accused while in the Detention Facility.[98]

130. Though no criminal record was included in the record, it is uncontested that the Accused had no prior criminal record. Accordingly, the Chamber finds that the Accused has no criminal convictions and will so note.

131. The certificate issued by the UNDF is a testimony to the good conduct of the Accused while in custody. The Chamber shall take such good conduct into consideration when determining the sentence.

2.4 Old age and sickness

(i) Submissions of the parties

132. The parties agree that the old age of the Accused, who is 60 years old, is a factor to be taken into account by the Chamber in determining the sentence.[99]

133. Both parties also submit that Vincent Rutaganira suffers from diabetes occasioning multiple harmful physiological effects and that he is afflicted with a partial permanent disability (15%) as a result of a motor vehicle accident.[100]

(ii) Discussion

134. The Chamber notes that in some cases, age was taken into account in determining sentence.[101]

---

[97] Simić Judgement (TC), para. 108; Nikolić Judgement (TC), para. 265.
[98] Ibid., para. 112. See also Krnojelac Judgement (TC), para. 520, and Krstić Judgement (TC), para. 715.
[99] Joint Brief, paras. 30-31.
[100] Ibid., para. 36.
[101] Erdemović II Judgement (TC), para. 16 (i); Furundžija Judgement (TC), par.284 ; Blaškić Judgement (TC), para. 778; Jugement Krnojelac Jugement (TC.), para. 533.

135. The Chamber notes that the medical report prepared by the Tribunal's Medical Officer does indeed confirm that Vincent Rutaganira is afflicted with Diabetes II and is in poor health.

136. It is the Chamber's view that, in the instant case, the advanced age of the Accused as well as the state of his health could be taken into account in determining his sentence.[102]

2.5 No active participation in the killings

(i) Submissions of the parties

137. The parties submit that Vincent Rutaganira did not participate actively in the killings in Mubuga secteur. He was merely accused of remaining in office at the time of the killings in 1994 and of failing to act so as to prevent or limit the scope of the massacres and atrocities committed at Mubuga.

(ii) Discussion

138. However, in the opinion of the Chamber, this goes to his criminal conduct rather than to mitigation.

3. Aggravating Circumstances

(i) Submissions of the Prosecution

139. The Prosecution submits that as the conseiller for Mubuga secteur, Vincent Rutaganira was a prominent member of his community.[103]

---

[102] PlavšićJudgement (TC), para. 106; Strugar Judgement (TC), para. 469.
[103] T.17 January 2005, p. 7.

140. The Accused was the closest person to the people in the secteur and was the bridge between the citizens and the local political structure "within the limits of his duties as set out in the relevant legislation governing his functions as conseiller". Such closeness to the local civilian population "placed him under a legal duty to espouse the principles laid down by the constitution of Rwanda and to uphold a higher than average degree of morality".[104]

141. It is the Prosecution's submission that given his level of education, Vincent Rutaganira, should know and appreciate the value and dignity of human life.[105] Vincent Rutaganira was therefore aware of the need for peaceful coexistence among the various components of the population in his secteur and should have promoted the virtues of tolerance.[106]

142. Lastly, the Prosecution submits that Vincent Rutaganira "took no active steps to protect the Tutsi refugees who had sought refuge inside the Mubuga church and, instead, literally stood aside and watched his fellow countrymen and women as they were slaughtered at the Mubuga parish church in April 1994".[107]

(ii) Discussion

142. [sic] The Chamber finds that some of the acts referred to above go to the Accused's criminal conduct rather than to aggravation.

143. The Chamber finds that that many women and children were killed in Mubuga Church is an aggravating circumstance.

---

[104] T.17 January 2005, p. 6.
[105] Idem.
[106] Ibid., pp. 6-7.
[107] Ibid., p. 7.

CIII05-0020 (E)

Translation certified by LSS, ICTR

4. Mitigating Circumstances

4.1 Voluntary surrender

(i) Submissions of the parties

144. The parties plead as a mitigating circumstance[108] the fact that Vincent Rutaganira voluntarily surrendered to the Tribunal on 18 February 2002,[109] after a warrant of arrest had been issued against him.

(ii) Discussion

145. The Chamber, in keeping with consistent case-law,[110] finds that Vincent Rutaganira's voluntary surrender to the Tribunal after a warrant of arrest had been issued against him is reflective of his respect for the international administration of justice. Therefore, the Chamber finds that his voluntary surrender is a mitigating circumstance.

4.2 Guilty plea

(i) Submissions of the parties

146. It is the submission of the parties that Vincent Rutaganira's guilty plea to Count 16 of the Indictment has resulted in judicial economy for the Tribunal and the international community in terms of financial resources and time. The parties submit that this reflects the Accused's willingness to contribute to the process of peace and national reconciliation in Rwanda.

---

[108] Joint Brief, 7 December 2004, para. 19.

[109] Guilty Plea Agreement, para. 32; Joint Brief, para. 20; [Joint motion for consideration of a plea agreement between Vincent Rutaganira and the Office of the Prosecutor before Trial Chamber III of the International Criminal Tribunal for Rwanda, 7 December 2004, para. 4.

[110] Strugar Judgement (TC), para. 472; Babić Judgement (TC), para. 86; Deronjic (TC), para. 266; Plavšić (TC), para. 107; Serushago Judgement (TC), para. 34.

(ii) Discussion

147. The Chamber notes that Vincent Rutaganira is only the fourth accused person to plead guilty before this Tribunal. In several cases, the Tribunal has held that a guilty plea should be considered as a mitigating circumstance.

148. In Serushago, the accused pleaded guilty to genocide and crimes against humanity. In light of his guilty plea, Serushago was sentenced to a single term of 15 years of imprisonment for all the crimes of which he has been convicted.[111] In Ruggiu, the accused pleaded guilty to the crime of direct and public incitement to commit genocide and of crime against humanity (persecution). Taking his guilty plea into account, the Chamber sentenced him to 12 years of imprisonment.[112]

149. In Erdemovic, the Trial Chamber of the International Criminal Tribunal for the Former Yugoslavia considered a guilty plea as a mitigating circumstance.[113]

150. In the light of such case-law of both ad hoc Tribunals, the Chamber finds that since a guilty plea is always an important factor in establishing the truth about a crime,[114] it should cause a reduction in the sentence that would have been otherwise handed down.[115]

151. However, the Chamber wishes to stress that a guilty plea serves public interest better if it is entered before the commencement or at the initial phase of the trial, thus enabling the Tribunal to save time and resources.[116]

---

[111] Serushago Judgement (TC). That sentence was confirmed on appeal. See The Prosecutor (The Respondent) v. Omar Serushago (The Appellant), Case No. ICTR-98-39-A, Judgement (appeal of sentence), 14 February 2000; and The Prosecutor (The Respondent) v. Omar Serushago (The Appellant), Case No. ICTR-98-39-A, Grounds of judgement, 6 April 2000.

[112] Ruggiu Judgement (TC), 1 June 2000.

[113] Erdemović Judgement II (TC), 5 March 1998, para. 16(ii). See also Erdemović Judgement (AC), Separate and dissenting opinion of Judge Antonio Cassese, para. 8.

[114] Banovic Judgement (TC), para. 68.

[115] Todorović Judgement (TC), para. 80.

[116] Idem. Todorović Judgement (TC), para. 81.

152. The Chamber, recalling that Vincent Rutaganira pleaded guilty before the commencement of the trial, finds that his guilty plea's contribution to the search for the truth must redound to his benefit. Accordingly, the Chamber will take such guilty plea into account in sentencing.

4.3 Assistance provided to certain victims

(i) Submissions of the parties

153. The parties agree that Vincent Rutaganira provided assistance to certain victims and saved their lives.

154. Witness TRV-4 testified that he was saved from death through Vincent Rutaganira's intervention.[117] Witness Immaculée Nyiramasimbi, the Accused's spouse, testified that she and her husband had hidden some Tutsi in their house for some weeks and, in particular, a woman who stayed for three months.[118]

(iii) Discussion

155. On this evidence which is not challenged especially by the Prosecution, and thus is judicially noticed, the Chamber finds that Vincent Rutaganira's assistance to persons targeted by attackers in their secteur should operate to mitigate his sentence.

4.4 Remorse

(i) Submissions of the parties

156. The parties agree that Vincent Rutaganira sincerely repented for having failed to act on behalf of the victims of the Mubuga Church massacre and that he is still remorseful for having failed to intervene in order to protect victims from the tragic events that took place in his secteur.[119]

---

[117] T.17 January 2005, pp. 20-21.
[118] Ibid., p. 26.
[119] Joint Brief, para. 28; Guilty Plea Agreement, para. 13.

157. The Chamber notes that, at his further initial appearance on 8 December 2004, Vincent Rutaganira expressed regret and asked for forgiveness as follows:

> "[as the conseiller for the secteur, I regret not being able to save the people who were at the church and I will never be able to forget the horror that I saw the day after the attacks that have left deep wounds in my heart. Once again, I ask for forgiveness from the families of the victims, and that is why I surrendered in order to tell the truth.]"[120]

158. The Chamber finds in mitigation that the expression of regret and remorse by the Accused is sincere.[121]

4.5 Duress

(i) Submissions of the parties

159. Both parties plead as a mitigating circumstance the real danger faced by Vincent Rutaganira or a member of his immediate family of being killed if the Accused had objected to the killings that were taking place in his secteur.[122]

160. The Defence prays the Chamber to take into consideration various statutes on failure to assist a person in danger and Article 31 of the Statute of the International Criminal Court.[123] The Defence submits that "[e]ach of those legislations considers a person guilty when that person fails to intervene, when he is in a position to do so without danger to himself. That means that the absolute danger is justification, absolute justification which excludes any guilt whatsoever".[124] The Defence also submits that the Chamber will have to weigh

[120] T.8 December 2004, p. 11.
[121] Strugar Judgement (TC), para. 471; Simić Judgement (TC), para. 94; Ruggiu Judgement (TC), paras. 69-72; Jokić Judgement (TC), para. 92; Nikolić Judgement (TC), para. 161; Todorović Judgement (TC), para. 92; Deronjić Judgement (TC), para. 264; Erdemović Judgement II (TC), para. 16 (iii).
[122] Joint Brief, para. 38; T.17 January 2005, p. 39. See statement of KPP1, T.17 January 2005, p. 31.
[123] Article 422 bis of the Belgian Penal Code; Article 49 of the Senegalese Penal Code; Article 593 of the Italian Penal Code; Article 223-6 of the French Penal Code; Article 256, para. 2, of the Rwandan Penal Code.
[124] T.17 January 2005, p. 39.

the real risk faced by the Accused and his family as a mitigating circumstance, taking into account "the proportionality that needs to be established between, on the one hand, that real danger, and on the other hand the legal duty, as a human being, in which the Accused failed and therefore pled guilty".[125]

(ii) Discussion

161. The Chamber fully endorses the finding by the Appeals Chamber of ICTY that "duress does not afford a complete defence to a soldier charged with a crime against humanity and/or war crime involving the killing of innocent human beings".[126] However, it is the Chamber's opinion that duress may be considered as a mitigating circumstance.[127]

162. The Chamber admits that there was duress in the instant case. In light of all the above, it finds that such duress goes to mitigation.

5. General practice regarding prison sentences in Rwanda

163. In determining the sentence to be imposed on the Accused, the Chamber will also review sentencing practice in Rwanda. Under the Statute and the Rules, such practice is but one of the factors to be taken into account by the Chamber in sentencing.[128]

164. Since the Statute and the Rules only provide for sentences of imprisonment, only such sentences will be taken into account in reviewing sentencing practice in Rwanda.

165. The Chamber notes several provisions of Organic Law No. 40/2000 of 26 January 2001 setting up "Gacaca courts" and organizing prosecutions for offences constituting the Crime of Genocide or Crimes against humanity,

---

[125] Idem.
[126] Erdemović Judgement (AC), para. 19.
[127] Erdemović Judgement II (TC), para. 17.
[128] Ruggiu Judgement (TC), para. 34; Serushago Judgement (TC), para. 18; Musema Judgement (TC), para. 984.

committed between 1 October 1990 and 31 December 1994. Such provisions are relevant pursuant to the lex mitior principle. Indeed, they provide for reduced sentences as compared to the law in force at the time the offence was committed, in particular, in respect of an accused who has pleaded guilty, and for commuting half of the imprisonment sentence to community service.

166. As regards specifically the plea procedure, the Chamber notes that it is provided for under Article 54 of the same Law in respect of "[anyone who committed the offences under Article 1]". However, under Article 55, only "persons in the 2nd, 3rd and 4th categories", who pleaded guilty "shall have their sentences commuted". The Chamber stresses that Vincent Rutaganira falls outside the first category under said Law. While the Chamber may not decide on commutation of imprisonment sentences, it will rely on the relevant provisions of the Rwandan Organic Law in determining the sentence.

C. Sentencing

167. Both parties submitted that they agreed to pray the Chamber to impose a sentence ranging from six to eight years of imprisonment, with Vincent Rutaganira being given credit for time spent in detention. Furthermore, the Defence prayed the Chamber not to sentence him to more than six years of imprisonment.[129] The Chamber reiterates that it has unfettered discretion in determining the appropriate sentence under the Statute and the Rules and that it is not bound by the parties' agreement, as acknowledged by both parties.[130]

[129] T.17 January 2005. p. 43.
[130] Guilty Plea agreement, para. 38.

1. Findings

168. In determining the appropriate sentence, the Chamber pursuant to the Statute and the Rules, reviewed factors to be taken into account in assessing the gravity of the crime of which Vincent Rutaganira was found guilty. It then considered the Accused's individual circumstances, and aggravating and mitigating circumstances. Lastly, it took account of the general practice regarding prison sentences in the courts of Rwanda.

169. Vincent Rutaganira is guilty of extermination as a crime against humanity, for having by omission, aided and abetted the massacre of thousands of Tutsi civilians who had taken refuge at Mubugu Church. The crime of extermination is particularly serious in light of the protected interests that were breached, that is, the lives and the physical and mental wellbeing of thousands of victims. That there were many women and children among the victims is an aggravating circumstance.

170. Vincent Rutaganira's guilty plea, his individual and family circumstances, his personality and conduct towards the Tutsi before and during the events, the absence of any criminal record and his good behaviour while in detention, the assistance he provided to some victims, his advanced age and illness, his voluntary surrender, the sincerity and the scope of his expression of remorse and the duress that weighed on him, are all factors that the Chamber considers as mitigating circumstances in determining the sentence.

2. Credit for time served

171. Vincent Rutaganira was arrested and transferred on 4 March 2002 to the United Nations Detention Facility in Arusha. He is entitled to credit for time spent in custody and any additional time he might spend in custody pending a final determination of a possible appeal.

CHAPTER VIII: DISPOSITION

FOR THESE REASONS,

THE TRIAL CHAMBER, delivering its judgement in public, inter partes and in the first instance, pursuant to the Statute and the Rules of Procedure and Evidence;

HAVING ORDERED the separation of the proceedings against the Accused Vincent Rutaganira from the other persons in the Indictment of 6 May 1996;

HAVING HEARD Vincent Rutaganira's guilty plea;

HAVING REVIEWED all the evidence as well as submissions by the parties;

ACQUITS Vincent Rutaganira on Counts 1, 14, 15, 17, 18 and 19 in the Indictment of 6 May 1996;

FINDS Vincent Rutaganira GUILTY of extermination as a crime against humanity for having aided and abetted, as an accomplice by omission, between 14 and 17 April 1994 or thereabouts, the massacres that took place at Mubuga Church in Gishyita commune, resulting in thousands of deaths and many wounded among the Tutsi refugees who were at said location;

SENTENCES the Accused Vincent Rutaganira to six years of imprisonment;

RULES that the sentence shall be enforced immediately;

RULES that pursuant to Rule 101(D) of the Rules, Vincent Rutaganira is entitled to credit for time spent in custody, to be computed from the date of his arrest, 4 March 2002, and any additional time he may spend in detention pending a final determination of a possible appeal;

RULES that pursuant to Rule 103(B) of the Rules, Vincent Rutaganira shall remain in the custody of the Tribunal pending finalization of arrangements for his transfer to the State where he shall serve his sentence.

Done in Arusha on 14 March 2005, in French and English, the French text being authoritative.

Andrésia Vaz	Flavia Lattanzi	Florence Rita Arrey
Presiding Judge	Judge	Judge

[Seal of the Tribunal]

CIII05-0020 (E)

Translation certified by LSS, ICTR